RAND ARROYO CENTER

T0099299

Identifying and Mitigating Risks in Security Sector Assistance for Africa's Fragile States

Stephen Watts

Prepared for the United States Army

For more information on this publication, visit www.rand.org/t/rr808

Library of Congress Cataloging-in-Publication Data is available for this publication.

ISBN 978-0-8330-8798-0

Published by the RAND Corporation, Santa Monica, Calif.

© Copyright 2015 RAND Corporation

RAND® is a registered trademark.

Support RAND
Make a tax-deductible charitable contribution at
www.rand.org/giving/contribute

www.rand.org

Preface

This research report presents an analysis of the risks inherent in U.S. security sector assistance to fragile states in Africa and how the United States might better anticipate and mitigate these risks. The findings reported here should be of interest to U.S. Army and U.S. Department of Defense planners and strategists as well as others interested in security sector assistance.

This research was sponsored by the Deputy Chief of Staff, G-8, U.S. Army, and conducted within the RAND Arroyo Center's Strategy and Resources Program. RAND Arroyo Center, part of the RAND Corporation, is a federally funded research and development center sponsored by the United States Army.

The Project Unique Identification Code (PUIC) for the project that produced this document is HQD126409.

Contents

Figure

Summary

State fragility in Africa affects multiple U.S. interests. Of greatest current concern to U.S. defense decisionmakers is the potential for transnational networks of violent extremist organizations, particularly those affiliated with al Qaeda and other Salafist terrorist networks, to flourish in these environments. The United States also is concerned by piracy, illicit trafficking (especially of narcotics, weapons, and people), access to critical resources (including oil and rare earth minerals), the potential for pandemic disease, and numerous humanitarian issues.

These varied interests, however, pose difficult trade-offs for U.S. decisionmakers generally and for the U.S. defense community in particular. The United States' current security priorities in Africa are (1) counterterrorism and (2) stabilizing partner nations, in part through increasing the capabilities of partner nations' security services to provide for their own security, consistent with the rule of law and human rights. In the long term, these priorities are mutually reinforcing. In the short term, they frequently conflict. The United States' need for access, intelligence, and other forms of cooperation with partner regimes in its counterterrorism efforts sometimes requires it to engage in forms of security sector assistance (SSA) that may have negative implications for these countries' long-term stability. Even in the absence of a counterterrorism agenda, the United States' wide-ranging interests will necessarily create trade-offs between long-term efforts to help strengthen and stabilize legitimate partners and more immediate priorities, whether those be securing troop contributions for peace operations, access for counterpiracy operations, diplomatic support for critical multilateral initiatives, or others.

These trade-offs imply that some degree of risk is inevitable. If such risks cannot be avoided, they must be openly acknowledged, evaluated, planned for, and—to the extent possible—mitigated through preventive action. Unfortunately, the U.S. government is currently ill prepared to engage in risk identification and mitigation for its SSA to the countries of Africa. Its SSA processes are scattered among a wide range of actors, with inadequate coordination between them. It currently lacks much of the information it would need to make fully informed decisions, and the analytic frameworks and interagency processes necessary to analyze this information and translate it into effective prevention and mitigation strategies are underdeveloped. Despite considerable progress in rationalizing the U.S. interagency process and in the monitoring and evaluation of SSA, much work remains to be done.

Findings

Although there are many areas of disagreement among them, quantitative studies on the aggregate effects of U.S. SSA have found them to be generally positive. They have also found, however, that these effects are highly conditioned by the types of assistance being offered and the characteristics of the partner nation, including its state reach, regime type (i.e., democracy or autocracy), and other characteristics. Material assistance (particularly arms transfers) has generally been found to be more problematic than assistance focused on training and education. Weak and autocratic states have difficulty making positive use of security sector assistance, and in many studies, such assistance was found to have potentially destabilizing effects.

While perhaps not surprising, these results pose a stark dilemma for those responsible for security sector assistance to the U.S. Africa Command (USAFRICOM) area of responsibility: The countries that are most in need of assistance are usually the ones least able to benefit from it. More specifically, the least stable countries typically possess weak and relatively undemocratic state institutions, and these countries have also been shown to make worse use of security sector assistance. The results are particularly problematic for many of the United States' closest counterterrorism partners in Africa, which are often governed by weak and relatively autocratic regimes.

These quantitative results are useful for establishing broad trends. They are less helpful for anticipating and mitigating specific risks. This report therefore also drew on the qualitative literature and extensive interviews to specify the precise ways in which security sector assistance might be destabilizing to fragile states. These "mechanisms" are summarized in the box below, although the list is not exhaustive.

Obviously, if U.S. security sector assistance is potentially destabilizing, this in itself is cause for concern. But the strategic implications of failed SSA policies extend beyond the direct and immediate consequences in the partner nation.

Perhaps most obviously, the United States risks being "tarred by the brush" of partner governments who act abusively toward their own populations. Even if the abusive behavior would have happened—or even been worse—in the absence of U.S. security sector assistance, the United States' reputation, both internationally and in the partner nation, can suffer.

Failures of security sector assistance can also have a negative impact on continued U.S. domestic support for such policies. France,

---

Mechanisms Through Which Security Sector Assistance May Destabilize the Domestic Politics of Fragile States

1. Undermining legitimate governance
   a. Creation of "praetorian guards"
   b. Eroding the principle of civilian supremacy
   c. Rent-seeking and nonresponsiveness
2. Exacerbating inter-communal tensions
   a. Shifting of inter-communal or inter-factional balance of power
   b. Internationalizing local conflicts
   c. Generating false perceptions
3. Diffusion of assistance to nonstate actors
   a. Diffusion of arms and other material assistance
   b. Diffusion of training and other nonmaterial assistance
4. Abetting abuses
5. Moral hazard

for instance, was forced to retrench from sub-Saharan Africa by the French public's opposition to military assistance in Africa after revelations of France's support to the Hutu regime in pregenocide Rwanda. Similarly, abuses by Salvadoran government forces during the war in El Salvador in the 1980s led the U.S. Congress to slash funding to that regime.

Finally, failures of security sector assistance often have subtler implications for the United States' ability to execute assistance policies elsewhere. The U.S. Agency for International Development (USAID), for instance, faced considerable restrictions on its support for foreign police services for many years in the wake of its support for abusive regimes in the 1960s and 1970s.

Policy Recommendations

The report offers four recommendations for improving the United States' ability to anticipate, plan for, and ultimately mitigate such risks—ones that the U.S. Departments of Defense and State can undertake without any changes to the legal or fiscal structure within which U.S. security sector assistance currently operates.

1. **Develop common "theories" of security sector assistance.** Before rigorous interagency planning or monitoring and evaluation can occur, the government requires "theories of change" that specify what changes the United States expects to see as a result of its assistance and why. Such "theories of change" have been adopted as a central component of much development assistance programming. They are government statements, somewhat analogous to military doctrine, about the expected results of given policies or programs, typically developed in substantial part on the basis of empirical research conducted by academic or other researchers using rigorous analytic methods. Without such "theories," it is simply impossible to know what exactly should be measured, and how, in any monitoring and evaluation effort, nor is it possible to account adequately for

second- and third-order consequences in planning processes. Currently the U.S. government lacks such "theories of change" for its SSA. Ongoing efforts to develop Army and Joint doctrine for security cooperation offer opportunities to incorporate such frameworks into U.S. Department of Defense (DoD) guidance. DoD should also incorporate such frameworks into its Guidance for Employment of the Force (GEF). DoD and the State Department should also include guidance along these lines in their country and regional strategies.

2. **Improve risk identification.** The systematic and documented identification and monitoring of risk is almost completely absent from U.S. SSA processes. The informal, intuitive approach to risk identification and monitoring generally adopted by the State Department is insufficient to this task. It is important to note that a wide range of development actors have found such informal approaches highly problematic, particularly in the context of fragile states, and have instead adopted formal assessment procedures. Numerous frameworks currently exist from which the United States could borrow to develop systematic procedures for identifying and monitoring risks. If it chose to do so, the United States also possesses many tools to collect data even in sensitive and insecure environments. The cost of such assessment efforts may well preclude their being conducted for partner nations that receive very small amounts of assistance. For those countries that receive more assistance (in the African context, particularly the recipients of Section 1206 funding), however, the costs of assessment are justified by the risks the United States accepts in offering such support.

3. **Improve planning to enable risk mitigation.** The United States could emphasize several risk-mitigation strategies in its planning for SSA to the fragile states of Africa. These measures include (1) incorporating the systematic identification and mitigation of the risk of political destabilization into the Integrated Country Strategies required by Presidential Policy Directive (PPD) 23, including the identification of possible "triggers" that would indicate when decisionmakers should review SSA for

possible termination; (2) focusing as much as possible on training and education activities, particularly in the early years of a
relationship as a means of gauging partner-nation commitment;
and (3) to the extent possible, developing incentive systems that
reward key personnel involved in SSA planning for outcomes
measured over the course of several years, not just in the one or
two years of their rotation cycles.

4. **Improve execution in ways that mitigate risks.** There are
    innumerable ways in which the United States could improve
    the execution of its SSA to mitigate its potential risks. A non-
    exhaustive list of such means includes (1) improving regional
    expertise among select uniformed personnel (beyond existing
    intensive investments in a small number of Foreign Area Offi-
    cers and fairly cursory regional training of personnel in Region-
    ally Aligned Forces) and incorporating risk analysis as a com-
    ponent of regional expertise and security cooperation training;
    (2) embedding U.S. forces in partners' ministries and with their
    forces where the partner nation is willing and the country rep-
    resents a high priority for the United States; and (3) better inte-
    grating contractors to ensure that their activities serve compre-
    hensive U.S. policy goals rather than narrow technical ones.

U.S. military planning emphasizes risk assessment and contingency planning. Similarly, the development community has put in
place many systematic frameworks for assessing partner-nation political structures and the potential for foreign assistance to inflame conflict in fragile states. Both the military and development communities
in recent years have placed much greater emphasis on program monitoring and evaluation. Despite these trends, formal assessment of risk
and planning for its mitigation is almost entirely absent from U.S. security sector assistance processes. This report suggests that the continued
absence of such procedures—of which many are already in existence
and relatively easy to adapt to security sector assistance—jeopardizes
U.S. efforts to achieve its goals in Africa and beyond, potentially at
significant cost to U.S. interests. Adopting risk assessment and mitigation practices will certainly not eliminate the risks of cooperating with

fragile regimes, but they offer a low-cost means of managing those risks while still pursuing critical U.S. goals.

Acknowledgments

The author appreciates the help and support offered by many individuals in the course of this study. In particular, I would like to thank Timothy Muchmore, the representative of the sponsoring office for this study, HQDA G-8.

The study also benefited immeasurably from the time and insights of the numerous people interviewed for it, particularly officials in the U.S. Department of Defense, U.S. Department of State, and U.S. Agency for International Development. Because most of these officials agreed to speak on a not-for-attribution basis, I cannot thank them by name, but I hope they will recognize their contributions to this report. I especially wish to thank Colonel Pedro G. Almeida, Chief of Staff, U.S. Army Africa (USARAF), who graciously hosted a visit by several of my RAND colleagues and me and allowed us to speak with his staff on a range of issues; Tim Hogan at USARAF, who facilitated contacts and arranged a very informative set of discussions; other officials at USAFRICOM, who made time for us despite the frequent fact-finding visits they receive; Michael Schwille, who worked tirelessly to set up invaluable meetings for me with the personnel of Combined Joint Task Force–Horn of Africa and others in Djibouti; and all personnel deployed in Africa who took time from their busy schedules to speak with me.

Finally, this report was greatly improved by comments and suggestions by the document's reviewers, Jefferson Marquis, Christopher Schnaubelt, and Brooke Stearns Lawson, and from Jason Campbell, LTC Marvin King, Michael McNerney, Karl Mueller, Olga Oliker,

Heather Peterson, and Stephanie Pezard. I am also grateful to my colleague Angel O'Mahony, who shared her quantitative data and expertise with me.

Abbreviations

AMISOM	African Union Mission in Somalia
AOR	area of responsibility
ATPUIC	Abbreviation Text Project Unique Identification Code
CAT	civil affairs team
DoD	Department of Defense
DRC	Democratic Republic of Congo
FMF	Foreign Military Financing
GEF	Guidance for Employment of the Force
HQDA	Headquarters, Department of the Army
IMET	International Military Education and Training
M&E	monitoring and evaluation
MoDA	Ministry of Defense Advisors
OECD	Organisation for Economic Co-operation and Development
PDD	Presidential Decision Directive
PME	professional military education
PPD	Presidential Policy Directive

PREACT	Partnership for Regional East Africa Terrorism
RCLF	regional, culture, and language familiarization
ROTC	Reserve Officer Training Corps
SCO	Security Cooperation Office
SSA	security sector assistance
SSR	security sector reform
TSCTP	Trans-Sahel Counterterrorism Partnership
USAFRICOM	U.S. Africa Command
USAID	U.S. Agency for International Development
USARAF	U.S. Army Africa
VEO	violent extremist organization

CHAPTER ONE

The Problem of Security Sector Assistance in Africa

Despite impressive economic growth in the past decade and some encouraging trends in governance, Africa remains dominated by fragile states. According to the Failed States Index, the four most fragile states in the world are all located in Africa, and more than two-thirds of all states in its bottom two categories are on the continent.[1]

State fragility in Africa touches on multiple U.S. interests. Of greatest current concern to U.S. defense decisionmakers is the potential for transnational networks of violent extremist organizations (VEOs), particularly those affiliated with al Qaeda and other Salafist terrorist networks, to flourish in these environments. The United States also is concerned by piracy, illicit trafficking (especially of narcotics, weapons, and people), access to critical resources (including oil and rare earth minerals), the potential for pandemic disease, and numerous humanitarian issues.[2]

These varied interests, however, pose difficult trade-offs for U.S. decisionmakers generally and for the U.S. defense community in particular. The United States' current security priorities in Africa are (1) counterterrorism and (2) stabilizing partner nations, in part through increasing the capabilities of partner nations' security services to provide for their own security, consistent with the rule of law and human

---

[1]   Fund for Peace, Failed States Index 2013, web page, 2013.

[2]   See, for instance, General Carter Ham, Commanding General, U.S. Africa Command, statement before the U.S. Senate Armed Services Committee, March 1, 2012 (hereafter referred to as the U.S. Africa Command Posture Statement), and White House, *U.S. Strategy Toward Sub-Saharan Africa,* June 2012.

rights. In the long term, these priorities may be mutually reinforcing. In the short term, there are frequent conflicts between them. The United States' need for access, intelligence, and other forms of cooperation with partner regimes in its counterterrorism efforts sometimes leads it to provide assistance—including security sector assistance (SSA)[3]— that may have negative implications for these countries' long-term stability. Even in the absence of a counterterrorism agenda, however, the United States' wide-ranging interests will necessarily create trade-offs between long-term efforts to help strengthen and stabilize legitimate partners and more immediate priorities.

These trade-offs imply that some degree of risk is inevitable. If such risks cannot be avoided, they must be openly acknowledged, evaluated, planned for, and—to the extent possible—mitigated through preventive action. Unfortunately, the United States government is currently ill-prepared to engage in risk identification and mitigation for its security sector assistance to the countries of Africa. Its security sector assistance processes are scattered among a wide range of actors, with inadequate coordination between them. It currently lacks much of the information it would need to make fully informed decisions, and the analytic frameworks and interagency processes necessary to analyze this information and translate it into effective prevention and mitigation strategies are underdeveloped. Despite considerable progress in rationalizing the U.S. interagency process and in monitoring and evaluation of security sector assistance, much work remains to be done.

Particularly in light of the Security Governance Initiative that the United States recently unveiled at the African Leadership Summit, it is critical to achieve the appropriate balance among competing U.S.

---

[3] Official terminology relating to U.S. cooperation with and assistance to foreign militaries can be highly confusing. Consistent with the recently issued Presidential Policy Directive (PPD) 23, "Security Sector Assistance," which provides the overarching policy guidance in this field, this report uses the term "security sector assistance" to encompass all forms of such cooperation and assistance, including those commonly referred to by the terms "security cooperation," "security assistance," "security force assistance," and "building partner capacity." Although the text of the PPD is not publicly available, the document is summarized in The White House, Office of the Press Secretary, "Fact Sheet: U.S. Security Sector Assistance Policy," April 5, 2013; and in the document "Implementation of Security Sector Assistance (SSA) Presidential Policy Directive (PPD)," undated.

priorities. This report explores the nature of the risks inherent in U.S. security cooperation with the fragile states of Africa and how the United States might better anticipate and mitigate these risks. More specifically, the report asks three central questions:

- What strategic risks does security sector assistance in the fragile states of Africa pose?
- Is the U.S. government currently well prepared to identify and mitigate those risks?
- To the extent it is not, what could be done at reasonable cost to improve U.S. policies and processes for identifying and mitigating risk?

It seeks to answer these questions in three steps. First, the United States' goals for engaging in security cooperation with countries in the U.S. Africa Command (USAFRICOM) area of responsibility (AOR) are reviewed, with a focus on the tensions between the United States' long-term stabilization goals and other interests.

Second is an examination of the potential risks posed by security sector assistance to fragile states. The report reviews the literature on the effects of security sector assistance, seeking to establish the dimensions of the problem, the precise channels through which foreign security assistance can have unintended and negative second- and third-order effects, and the challenges that such unintended consequences have posed to U.S. and allied governments in the past. This literature review encompasses both quantitative and qualitative research and wherever possible identifies points of agreement between multiple reports.

Third, the U.S. process for approving, planning, executing, and reviewing security cooperation and security sector assistance is investigated more generally. This section includes suggestions for improving risk identification and mitigation processes in the development, execution, and review of U.S. security cooperation and security sector assistance.

Trade-Offs Among U.S. Policy Goals in Africa

Over the past decade, a growing consensus has emerged among experts in both the academic and policy worlds that the responsible strengthening of African security services must be a part of a holistic approach to Africa's troubles, alongside efforts to promote equitable economic development and improvements in governance.[4] Indeed, many have argued that reforms of African security services are critical to addressing issues of poverty and poor governance that afflict the continent.[5]

This growing consensus coincides with a movement within the U.S. defense community to emphasize preventive uses of security cooperation. The 2012 Defense Strategic Guidance, for instance, states

> Across the globe we will seek to be the security partner of choice, pursuing new partnerships with a growing number of nations—including those in Africa and Latin America—whose interests and viewpoints are merging into a common vision of freedom,

---

[4]   On the importance of security sector reform in Africa, see, for instance, Andre Le Sage, "Africa's Irregular Security Threats: Challenges for U.S. Engagement," Strategic Forum No. 255, Washington, D.C.: Institute for National Strategic Studies, May 2010; Jeffrey Herbst, "African Militaries and Rebellion: The Political Economy of Threat and Combat Effectiveness," *Journal of Peace Research*, Vol. 41, No. 3, May 2004, pp. 357–369; Nicole Ball, Piet Biesheuvel, Tom Hamilton-Baillie, and 'Funmi Olonisakin, *Security and Justice Sector Reform Programming in Africa*, Evaluation Working Paper 23, London: UK Department for International Development, April 2007; and Daniel Bendix and Ruth Stanley, "Security Sector Reform in Africa: The Promise and the Practice of a New Donor Approach," Durban, South Africa: *ACCORD* Occasional Paper Series, Vol. 3, No. 2, 2008. On its importance more generally, see Nicole Ball, *Promoting Security Sector Reform in Fragile States*, PPC Issue Paper No. 11, Washington, D.C.: U.S. Agency for International Development, April 2005; Monica Duffy Toft, *Securing the Peace: The Durable Settlement of Civil Wars*, Princeton, N.J.: Princeton University Press, 2010; International Dialogue on Peacebuilding and Statebuilding, *The Monrovia Roadmap on Peacebuilding and Statebuilding*, July 2011; and Organisation for Economic Co-operation and Development Development Assistance Committee 2012, "Building Blocks to Prosperity: The Peacebuilding and Statebuilding Goals (PSGs)," Paris, 2012.

[5]   See, for instance, Ball, 2005, pp. 2, 5–6; Bendix and Stanley, 2009, pp. 9–10; Herbst, 2004, p. 367; Global Facilitation Network for Security Sector Reform, *A Beginner's Guide to Security Sector Reform (SSR)*, Birmingham, UK, 2007, p. 4; United Nations Development Programme, *Security Sector Reform and Transitional Justice: A Crisis Post-Conflict Programmatic Approach*, New York, 2003, p. 13.

stability, and prosperity. Whenever possible, we will develop innovative, low-cost, and small-footprint approaches to achieve our security objectives, relying on exercises, rotational presence, and advisory capabilities.[6]

Similarly, the USAFRICOM Posture Statement states, "We will strive to build upon existing relationships and develop new partnerships in Africa in order to strengthen the defense capabilities of partner nations to better enable them to provide for their own security while increasingly contributing to regional security and stability."[7] Such efforts are based on the assumption, made explicit in multiple U.S. strategic guidance documents, that U.S. efforts to help foreign countries govern and defend themselves in ways that respect the rule of law and human rights ultimately advance U.S. strategic interests.[8]

This apparent congruence between Africa experts' policy prescriptions for stabilizing the continent and U.S. Department of Defense (DoD) strategic guidance suggests the potential for DoD and the U.S. Army in particular to play an important role in Africa's future. Beneath this surface-level congruence, however, lie major differences of approach that imply significant risks for both the United States and its African partners.

Experts on Africa and on conflict generally support the "security sector reform" (SSR) paradigm, which emphasizes the simultaneous development of both security capabilities and oversight and accountability mechanisms to ensure the legitimate functioning of those capabilities.[9] SSR programs seek to engage a wide variety of actors, includ-

---

[6] U.S. Department of Defense, *Sustaining U.S. Global Leadership: Priorities for 21st Century Defense,* Washington, D.C., January 2012, p. 3.

[7] USAFRICOM Posture Statement (Ham, 2012), p. 1.

[8] See especially the White House, 2012; see also White House, *National Security Strategy,* 2010, and White House, *National Strategy for Counterterrorism,* June 2011. See also Greg Mills "Africa's New Strategic Significance," *Washington Quarterly,* Vol. 27, No. 4, 2004, pp. 164–165.

[9] The canonical document on security sector reform remains the Organisation for Economic Co-Operation and Development ECD Development Assistance Committee, *Handbook on Security System Reform: Supporting Security and Justice,* Paris, 2007. On Africa specifi-

ing parliamentarians and civil society, in ensuring that security forces are the servants of the population, not the regime. Proponents of SSR argue that capacity-building efforts without the simultaneous development of oversight and accountability mechanisms are likely to backfire, ultimately creating greater instability.

Unfortunately, many less-than-democratic regimes find such reform programs highly threatening: They often build their security forces and civil-military institutions around the imperative of regime preservation rather than on the basis of broader popular accountability.[10] As a result, they either reject out of hand any capacity-building assistance that is predicated on the SSR paradigm or, if they are highly dependent on international assistance, they may accept the capacity-building assistance while subverting any efforts at building democratic oversight and accountability. For this reason, the SSR paradigm has struggled to adapt to circumstances other than the two for which it was initially developed—instances of post-conflict and democratic transitions.[11] Similarly, SSR's (appropriate) focus on long-term change often

---

cally, see, for instance, Mills, 2004, p. 165; Eric Bonnemaison, "Security Sector Planning in Africa: Military Force as a Public Good," *African Security Review*, Vol. 11, No. 2, 2002; and Herbert M. Howe, *Ambiguous Order: Military Forces in African States*, Boulder, Colo.: Lynne Rienner Publishers, 2001.

[10] For an overview of this phenomenon in Africa, see Howe, 2001. On the importance of political inclusion—both within and outside of security services—for the stability of conflict-affected states more generally, see Stephen Watts, Jason H. Campbell, Patrick B. Johnston, Sameer Lalwani, and Sarah H. Bana, *Countering Others' Insurgencies: Understanding U.S. Small-Footprint Interventions in Local Context*, Santa Monica, Calif.: RAND Corporation, RR-513-SRF, 2014.

[11] Albrecht Schnabel, "Ideal Requirements Versus Real Environments in Security Sector Reform," *Security Sector Reform in Challenging Environments*, Geneva: Geneva Centre for the Democratic Control of Armed Forces (DCAF), 2009; Mark Sedra, "Security Sector Reform in Afghanistan and Iraq: Exposing a Concept in Crisis," *Journal of Peacebuilding and Development*, Vol. 3, No. 2, 2007, pp. 7–23; and Andrew Mackay, Mark Sedra, and Geoff Burt, "Security Sector Reform (SSR) in Insecure Environments: Learning from Afghanistan," *Journal of Security Sector Management*, Vol. 8, No. 3, September 2011, pp. 1–20. The High-Level Forum on African Perspectives on SSR and Experts-Level Seminar on African Perspectives on SSR recognized both the importance of applying SSR more broadly and some of the challenges; see High-Level Forum on African Perspectives on SSR and Experts-Level Seminar on African Perspectives on SSR, *African Perspectives on Security Sector Reform*, New York: United Nations, May 14, 2010.

leaves practitioners ill prepared for responding to shorter-term security demands.

At a declaratory level, the United States has committed itself to emphasizing SSR principles in its security sector assistance, both globally and specifically in Africa.[12] In practice, the relationship between SSR and U.S. security sector assistance policies is much more complex.

The United States has a broader range of goals than those underlying SSR. The SSR paradigm emphasizes long-term human security goals in the partner nation. The United States pursues such goals, but these goals must compete with others. Besides seeking to build the capabilities of partner nations to provide for their own security, the United States often seeks access rights so that its forces can respond effectively to contingencies, information and intelligence on regional dynamics, and influence over a wide range of issues with the decision-makers of partner states (including participation in multilateral operations, passage of counterterrorism legislation, support for U.S. initiatives in intergovernmental institutions such as the United Nations, and so on).

In the African context, tensions between long-term stability and other goals are most acute in the case of the U.S. counterterrorism agenda, although they are present elsewhere as well.[13] The United States, for instance, recently decided to base remotely piloted aircraft ("drones") in Niger in order to conduct surveillance of violent extremist organizations in neighboring Mali and elsewhere in the Sahel. The U.S. move has been described as an important contribution to the French-led intervention in Mali that has restored some degree of peace

---

[12] This commitment is most explicit in the document *Security Sector Reform* (U.S. Agency for International Development, U.S. Department of Defense, U.S. Department of State, *Security Sector Reform,* February 2009). Many SSR principles are also at the core of the newly issued PPD 23, "Security Sector Assistance." The USAFRICOM Posture Statement also adopts the language of SSR (without ever using the term explicitly) when it declares, "We focus on the development of professional militaries which are disciplined, capable, and responsible to civilian authorities and committed to the well being of their citizens and protecting human rights" (Ham, 2012, p. 5).

[13] For one former U.S. ambassador's reflections on the tensions between the United States' counterterrorism and other agendas in Africa, see David H. Shinn, "Walking the Line: U.S. Security Policy in East Africa and the Horn," *World Politics Review*, February 20, 2013.

to that country, but observers have warned that the drone access rights may exacerbate long-standing ethnic tensions in Niger.[14] In another case, the United States provides considerable security sector assistance to the Ugandan People's Defense Force, in large part because of its leading role in the African Union Mission in Somalia (AMISOM). By many accounts, AMISOM has played a very positive role in reducing levels of violence in Somalia, extending the Somali federal government's reach and reducing the threat posed by the Islamist militant group al Shabaab.[15] To ensure Uganda's continuing commitment to this effort, however, the United States has had to provide security sector assistance to an autocratic regime.[16] Such regimes are clearly beyond the scope of most conceptions of security sector reform, which focus on democratic accountability, and military cooperation with such regimes can sometimes endanger U.S. relationships with their successors.[17]

On the whole, U.S. security sector assistance to Africa has been so low in most of the post–Cold War era that it has had little chance to make a major impact, either positive or negative. The primary exception is funding for major U.S. counterterrorism partners. Uganda, Burundi, Mauritania, and Tunisia, for instance, all have been in the highest tier of Section 1206 (counterterrorism) assistance recipients in recent years, each receiving tens of millions of dollars.[18] For countries such as

---

[14] See, for instance, Eric Schmitt, "Drones in Niger Reflect New U.S. Tack on Terrorism," *New York Times*, July 10, 2013. Given the reputation of U.S. drones, particularly in the Muslim world, the introduction even of unarmed drones risks some degree of "blowback."

[15] See, for instance, Matt Bryden, *Somalia Redux? Assessing the New Somali Federal Government,* Center for Strategic and International Studies, Lanham, Md.: Rowman and Littlefield, August 2013.

[16] On the Ugandan-donor relationship, see Jonathan Fisher, "Managing Donor Perceptions: Contextualizing Uganda's 2007 Intervention in Somalia," *African Affairs*, Vol. 111, No. 444, 2012, pp. 404–423.

[17] On the long-term foreign policy consequences of military assistance to authoritarian regimes, see Ely Ratner, "Reaping What You Sow: Democratic Transitions and Foreign Policy Realignment," *Journal of Conflict Resolution*, Vol. 53, No. 3, June 2009, pp. 390–418. Examples include the Philippines in the Marcos era and Iran in the era of the Shah.

[18] Nina M. Serafino, *Security Assistance Reform: "Section 1206" Background and Issues for Congress,* Washington, D.C.: Congressional Research Service, April 4, 2014, p. 6.

Burundi and Uganda (both major troop contributors to AMISOM) or Mauritania (a key counterterrorism partner in the Sahel region), U.S. security sector assistance in 2012 was equivalent to roughly one-fifth of these countries' defense budgets.[19]

When the United States pursues short-term objectives such as counterterrorism goals at some risk to its goal of promoting long-term stability, it is not simply a case of short-sightedness or irrationally discounting the future. In many cases the potential for small security sector reform programs to make a meaningful contribution to a fragile state's long-term stability is extremely small, as the next chapter will discuss in greater detail. Similarly, many of the more dire predictions of "blowback" or destabilization made by critics of U.S. security policies in Africa have not transpired. If the probability of long-term negative consequences is relatively small, and the probability of attaining short-term goals is quite large, then pocketing small gains in the short term may be justified, even at the expense of some long-term risk. The problem is that the United States lacks the information and mechanisms necessary to weigh these trade-offs systematically.

---

[19] Data on these countries' defense budgets come from International Institute for Strategic Studies, *The Military Balance*, Vol. 113, No. 1, 2013.

CHAPTER TWO

Risks of SSA in the Fragile States of Africa

U.S. Army and Joint doctrine call for the anticipation and mitigation of risk and the development of branches and sequels in operational plans in case operations do not transpire as anticipated. Yet the Army doctrinal manual on security cooperation devotes less than a page of text to risk mitigation. Risk, moreover, is understood in extremely narrow terms, either as the potential for security cooperation activities to negatively influence other countries, or as the potential for narrowly defined operational objectives to go unfulfilled. This chapter explores the potential risks that SSA activities can pose to the long-term stability of fragile partner states. It does so first by reviewing the quantitative literature on the relationship between SSA and various indicators of partner-nation stability and political development. These quantitative studies are useful for discerning broad trends. They are limited, however, in their ability to distinguish more nuanced causal relationships. Consequently, the next section attempts to specify particular paths by which SSA may threaten partner-nation stability. A final section discusses potential strategic implications for the United States. The goal is not to make any summary judgments about the overall impact of SSA; as the following discussion emphasizes, the impact of SSA is highly context-specific. Rather, the intent is to help develop a broader appreciation of the manifold consequences of security cooperation in an effort to inform Army planning and review processes—a topic to which the discussion will return in the final two chapters of this report.

Quantitative Assessments of SSA Effects on Partner Stability

There have been relatively few rigorous quantitative assessments of the effects of U.S. security sector assistance on partner nations' stability and political development. Much work remains to be done in specifying the impact of U.S. assistance more precisely and better discerning causality. Nonetheless, these studies do suggest a number of important trends, particularly once the characteristics of particular partner nations and types of U.S. security assistance are taken into account.

Perhaps the best single study of U.S. security sector assistance is a recent RAND report designed to assess the ability of such programs to prevent outbreaks of violent conflict. The analysis examined the relationship between U.S. security sector assistance and a partner nation's stability, measured using the State Fragility Index. The report finds a statistically significant positive relationship between U.S. security sector assistance and improvement in partner nations' stability. Importantly, this relationship is strongly conditioned by both the nature of the security sector assistance and the characteristics of the partner nation. Smaller-scale programs, particularly those focused on educating the leaders of partner-nation militaries, are shown to be most effective, while Foreign Military Financing (FMF) may have negative effects (although the relationship between FMF and changes in stability is not strong enough to achieve statistical significance). U.S. security sector assistance appears to have no statistically significant effect on the stability of fragile and weak states; in the weakest states, the relationship is actually negative (although, again, not statistically significant). Finally, while U.S. assistance has had clearly positive effects in Latin America, East Asia, and Europe, it has had no statistically significant positive effect on stability in Africa or the Middle East, and the relationship is again negative (although not statistically significant) in North Africa and the Middle East.

Many other quantitative studies have yielded findings that are consistent with the general patterns in the RAND analysis, although there is little consensus in the field, and even where patterns are similar, the studies often differ in the details. One academic study found that

military-to-military contacts between U.S. and partner-nation personnel increased the likelihood of partner-nation democratization, and
another found that partner nations' participation in U.S. professional
military education (PME) programs decreased the likelihood that
these partner nations would experience a coup. In contrast, another
study found the opposite—that U.S.-provided PME increased the likelihood of coups.

There are many reasons why these studies may have come to different conclusions. In part, the divergent conclusions may be the result
of different outcomes of interest: One study measured the effects of
assistance on stability, another on democratization, and two others on
coups. Moreover, the time periods covered by the various studies are
different. Generally speaking, the studies were more likely to find positive effects from U.S. security sector assistance if their data drew more
heavily on the post–Cold War era. Finally, the studies all treated contextual factors (such as levels of development, regime type, and so on)
differently.

Several other studies have examined the relationship between
arms transfers and political dynamics in recipient countries. Consistent with the findings of the RAND study, two different studies found
positive and statistically significant relationships between the scale of
arms transfers and the likelihood of human rights abuses, the probability of coups, and the length of military rule. Interestingly, a third study
finds that arms transfers depress the likelihood of coups in the short
term, ostensibly by meeting the military's demands for greater capabilities, but increases the likelihood of coups in the long term as the
military becomes an ever-stronger actor in domestic politics. Unfortunately, all of these studies used data predominantly from the Cold
War period, so it is possible that the relationship between arms transfers and political outcomes has changed in the post–Cold War period
(although the results of the RAND study suggest this is not the case).
The studies also used either no control variables for state capacity and
fragility or highly incomplete ones, and they did not examine the inter-
active effects of arms transfers with these contextual variables. It may
be that arms transfers are unproblematic among highly capable and
democratic states but have much more negative consequences in fragile

states. Such a relationship would again be consistent with the RAND study, but these other analyses do not allow us to test the robustness of that relationship.

It should probably come as no surprise that the effects of U.S. security sector assistance are highly conditioned by the characteristics of the partner nation, including its state reach (that is, the capacity of the regime to provide public goods throughout its territory), regime type (i.e., democracy or autocracy), and other characteristics. Numerous studies have found that these characteristics shape the likelihood that regimes will engage in human rights abuses, mass killings, and genocide. They also exercise strong effects on these regimes' stability.

While perhaps not surprising, these results pose a stark dilemma for those responsible for U.S. security sector assistance to the USAFRICOM area of responsibility: The countries that are most in need of assistance are usually the ones least able to make positive use of it (that is, to improve their levels of stability). To help illustrate the problem, Figure 2.1 indicates which countries score low enough on indicators of state reach to suggest that U.S. security assistance might have negative consequences on their stability, according to the analysis of the RAND study referenced previously. Unfortunately, these countries of concern coincide remarkably closely with the United States' priority partners for counterterrorism—the countries of the Trans-Sahel Counterterrorism Partnership (TSCTP) and the Partnership for Regional East Africa Terrorism (PREACT).

Mechanisms Through Which Security Cooperation Can Have Destabilizing Effects

The quantitative results described in the previous section are useful for establishing broad trends. They have two weaknesses, however. First, through such large, cross-national analyses, it is nearly impossible to be certain if the positive correlation observed is the consequence of U.S. assistance, or if it is instead only the consequence of the United States' choosing its partners or its type of assistance wisely. If the latter is true,

Figure 2.1
Countries of Concern for Security Sector Assistance in USAFRICOM

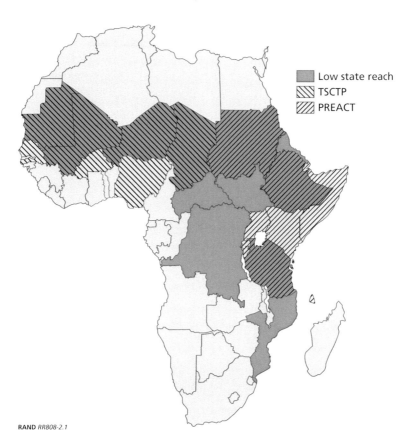

- Low state reach
- TSCTP
- PREACT

RAND *RR808-2.1*

then expanded use of SSA might have negative outcomes. Second, such studies are less helpful for anticipating and mitigating specific risks.

In an effort to address these two limitations, this section draws on the qualitative literature to specify the precise ways in which security sector assistance might destabilize the domestic politics of fragile states. These "mechanisms" are summarized in the box below, although the list is not exhaustive. Wherever possible, this section uses multiple sources written by Africa regional experts and invokes multiple examples to suggest the plausibility of these mechanisms. They are nonetheless offered not as proven facts, but rather as credible hypotheses.

Mechanisms Through Which Security Sector Assistance May Destabilize the Domestic Politics of Fragile States

1. Undermining legitimate governance
   a. Creation of "praetorian guards"
   b. Eroding the principle of civilian supremacy
   c. Rent-seeking and nonresponsiveness
2. Exacerbating inter-communal tensions
   a. Shifting of inter-communal or inter-factional balance of power
   b. Internationalizing local conflicts
   c. Generating false perceptions
3. Diffusion of assistance to nonstate actors
   a. Diffusion of arms and other material assistance
   b. Diffusion of training and other nonmaterial assistance
4. Abetting abuses
5. Moral hazard

The number of these mechanisms and the frequency with which Africa experts have highlighted them suggest that they are worthy of systematic risk identification and mitigation processes in the U.S. government, even if alternative explanations may be identified for any individual case.

Undermining Legitimate Governance

Despite the United States' emphasis on using its education programs to instill appropriate civil-military values in partner-nation military officers, security sector assistance poses some potential to weaken partner-nation governance.

Perhaps the most obvious risk is the inadvertent creation or strengthening of "praetorian guards"—that is, elite forces whose loyalty is to an autocrat, party, or ethnic group in power, rather than to the state as a whole, and whose actions are not governed by the rule of law. Such parallel forces are common throughout Africa.[1] Protecting a legitimate regime against violent challengers is a fully appropriate role for U.S. security assistance. But if forces loyal to a particular leader become so powerful that the leader need not fear any challenge—including challenges posed by ordinary democratic practices such as elections— then they pose a threat to the U.S. concept of legitimate governance. In

---

[1]   Howe, 2001.

most cases, U.S. security sector assistance in Africa is not large enough to create such "praetorian guards," although it may help to sustain them through training, equipment, and advice. Particularly in poor countries that are the beneficiaries of substantial U.S. counterterrorism assistance (or, as in Latin America, counter-drug assistance), the influx of resources poses some degree of risk in this regard. In impoverished Mauritania, for instance, some regional experts have maintained that U.S. counterterrorism support—both by providing material resources to units "at the core of the regime's security apparatus" and by providing symbolic support for the regime—provided an important crutch that permitted a previous regime to take undemocratic actions.[2]

More subtly, security sector assistance can shift power and resources to security services and away from the civilian institutions meant to provide oversight and accountability over these services. Extremely large infusions of resources to the security sector make the security services the major source of patronage. In extreme cases such as South Vietnam, these services become more powerful actors than the civilians ostensibly in charge.[3] Similarly, to the extent security sector assistance improves the organizational capacity of the military and other security institutions, it may make these bodies the most cohesive, capable actors in extremely weak states.[4] Again, in the case of Africa,

---

[2] Cédric Jourde, "Constructing Representations of the 'Global War on Terror' in the Islamic Republic of Mauritania," *Journal of Contemporary African Studies*, Vol. 25, No. 1, 2007, p. 94; see also Cédric Jourde, "Sifting Through the Layers of Insecurity in the Sahel: The Case of Mauritania," Africa Security Brief No. 15, Africa Center for Strategic Studies, National Defense University, September 2011; and Princeton N. Lyman, "The War on Terrorism in Africa," Donald Rothchild and John W. Harbeson, eds., *Africa in World Politics*, Boulder, Colo.: Westview Press, 2013.

[3] See, for instance, Sir Robert Thompson, *Defeating Communist Insurgency: The Lessons of Malaya and Vietnam*, St. Petersburg, Fla.: Hailer Publishing, 2005 [1966], pp. 58–59.

[4] John Samuel Fitch, "The Political Impact of U.S. Military Aid to Latin America: Institutional and Individual Effects," *Armed Forces and Society*, Vol. 5, 1979, pp. 360–386. Critics of U.S. policy in Mali have made essentially this argument in relation to the coup launched by the U.S.-trained Captain Amadou Sanogo; see, for instance, Simon Tisdall, "Mali: Fragile Democracy and Clumsy U.S. Policy," *The Guardian*, January 18, 2013. These arguments, however, have thus far failed to make a compelling case that U.S.-imparted skills or other capabilities were a *cause* of the Malian coup.

the amount of security sector assistance is seldom large enough to completely alter power dynamics by itself. It can, however, make security services less dependent on civilian authorities for their resources and, thus, less accountable and potentially more assertive and even abusive.[5]

Finally, particularly when substantial amounts of aid are involved, assistance runs the risk of exacerbating "rentier-state" dynamics even if the civil-military balance is not disturbed. Many observers have noted that aid is fungible, at least to some degree—that is, aid provided for one function frees up funds that the partner government may have had to spend on that function.[6] The partner government, in turn, is free to spend the newly available funds on whatever it may choose—including the financing of unproductive activities intended to strengthen its patronage networks or otherwise secure its control. To the extent the partner government is not reliant on its own citizens for revenues but can instead rely on outside aid to "buy" support, it need not be responsive to popular demands. Such "rentier states" run high risks of poor governance.[7]

Exacerbating Inter-Communal Tensions

A second set of mechanisms through which security sector assistance can have destabilizing effects concerns the potential of such assistance to inflame inter-communal tensions. Many Africa specialists

---

[5]   Stephen Ellis, "Briefing: The Pan-Sahel Initiative," *African Affairs*, Vol. 103, No. 412, pp. 459–464; Cédric Jourde, "The International Relations of Small Neoauthoritarian States: Islamism, Warlordism, and the Framing of Stability," *International Studies Quarterly*, Vol. 51, 2007, pp. 481–503; for similar dynamics elsewhere, see also Yezid Sayigh, *Policing the People, Building the State: Authoritarian Transformation in the West Bank and Gaza*, Washington, D.C.: Carnegie Endowment for International Peace, February 2011.

[6]   See, for instance, Tarhan Feyzioglu, Vinaya Swaroop, and Min Zhu, "A Panel Data Analysis of the Fungibility of Foreign Aid," *World Bank Economic Review*, Vol. 12, No. 1, 1998, pp. 29–58; and Nasir M. Khilji and Ernest M. Zampelli, "The Fungibility of U.S. Military and Non-Military Assistance and the Impacts on Expenditures of Major Aid Recipients," *Journal of Development Economics*, Vol. 43, No. 2, April 1994, pp. 345–362.

[7]   Deborah Bräutigam, *Aid Dependence and Governance*, Stockholm: Expert Group on Development Issues, 2000; Nicolas van de Walle, *African Economies and the Politics of Permanent Crisis, 1979–1999*, New York: Cambridge University Press, 2001; World Bank, *Assessing Aid: What Works, What Doesn't, and Why*, Washington, D.C.: World Bank, 1998.

have warned that foreign security assistance has shifted the balance of power between different ethnic or confessional groups in highly fragile states. The two most commonly cited examples are the polarization of Christian-Muslim relations in Kenya and the disruption of informal power-sharing arrangements in Mali and Niger. In Kenya, several regional specialists have warned that U.S. security sector assistance and U.S. pressure on the Kenyan government to crack down on suspected terrorist targets have led to an increase in abusive behavior by Kenyan security services against the country's Muslim minority.[8] In Mali and Niger, the United States has attempted to disrupt illicit trading routes through the Sahara by strengthening the border-monitoring and enforcement capabilities of those countries' governments. Many Africa experts have warned that these U.S. efforts have had the effect of cutting off vital revenue streams to Tuareg communities, which Bamako and Niamey had previously tacitly accepted as a form of "parasovereign" power-sharing designed to calm tensions with their Tuareg populations.[9]

Even if U.S. security sector assistance does little to change objective power relations between different groups, it can fuel misperceptions and suspicions in partner countries. One regional specialist described how even small-scale U.S. security cooperation activities were seized upon by local actors looking to promote their own agendas by inflaming inter-communal tensions:

> The shadowy American military presence in the region has thus more recently become a key object of rampant rumor and speculation, used again by a variety of Muslim leaders competing in a larger Saharan moral economy, from Songhay and Bellah to

[8]   Beth Elise Whitaker, "Reluctant Partners: Fighting Terrorism and Promoting Democracy in Kenya," *International Studies Perspectives*, Vol. 9, 2008, pp. 254–271; Jan Bachmann and Jana Hönke, "'Peace and Security' as Counterterrorism? The Political Effects of Liberal Interventions in Kenya," *African Affairs*, Vol. 109, No. 434, 2009, pp. 97–114.

[9]   Ellis, 2004; Robert G. Berschinski, *AFRICOM's Dilemma: The "Global War on Terrorism," "Capacity Building," Humanitarianism, and the Future of U.S. Security Policy in Africa,* Carlisle Barracks, Pa.: Strategic Studies Institute, U.S. Army War College, 2007, pp. 30–31; David Gutelius, "Islam in Northern Mali and the War on Terror," *Journal of Contemporary African Studies*, Vol. 25, No. 1, 2007, pp. 59–76; Jourde, 2007.

Kunta and Kel Ifoghas. Here the truth of a claim is measured not in absolute terms, but rather in how well these claims fit the perceptions and a priori understanding of listeners. Rumors of inappropriate conduct by US personnel began to spread in the north [of Mali] through 2004 and public statements by American military leaders, interpreted and rebroadcast by northern political leaders, have added to resentment among northern leaders.[10]

Similar misperceptions and conspiracy theories have flourished in Somalia as a result of U.S. activities.[11]

Not all misperceptions occur among a misinformed populace; they are also possible among government officials. Close security cooperation between the United States and partner-nation leaders may cause those leaders to believe that the United States will support any of their actions, so long as they are undertaken in the name of counterterrorism or another security agenda prioritized by the United States.[12] The United States might thus be perceived to be providing a "green light" to repressive activities or coups d'état, even if the United States in fact later cuts off aid to punish such activities.

Diffusion of Assistance to Nonstate Actors

A third area of concern lies in the potential for U.S. security sector assistance—either material assistance or training—to end up in the hands of nonstate actors. Such diffusion of U.S. assistance has happened elsewhere in the world. Cold War–era U.S. armaments such as grenades have escaped the armories of El Salvador and Guatemala and wound up in the hands of Mexican drug cartels.[13] Similarly, U.S.-trained Mexican special forces have reportedly defected to the feared

---

[10] Gutelius, 2007, p. 68.

[11] Peter J. Quaranto, *Building States While Fighting Terror: Contradictions in United States Strategy in Somalia from 2001 to 2007*, ISS Monograph Series No. 143, Pretoria, South Africa: Institute for Security Studies (ISS), May 2008, p. 55.

[12] See, for instance, Jourde, 2007.

[13] Colby Wilkason and Mikhaila Fogel, "Cartel Weapons and Their Provenance," *The War on Mexican Cartels: Options for U.S. and Mexican Policy-Makers,* Cambridge, Mass.: Harvard University Institute of Politics, September 2012, p. 29.

Los Zetas cartel.[14] In other cases, U.S. military assistance has allegedly been transferred from partner militaries to paramilitary groups engaged in extrajudicial killings.[15]

In Africa, analogous occurrences have been reported. One report, for instance, claimed that the entire Niger Rapid Intervention Company, trained by U.S. forces, had defected to Tuareg insurgents.[16] U.S.-trained Malian government forces also reportedly defected to join Tuareg insurgent groups in that country.[17] Sometimes the diversion of U.S. assistance is much more subtle. In Kenya, for example, observers have worried that U.S.-provided intelligence and other capabilities are more likely to be used by Kenyan security services in various criminal enterprises than to be used for the counterterrorism purposes for which they were intended.[18]

Abetting Abuses

Perhaps the risk most feared by the United States is that its security sector assistance may be used in the perpetration of large-scale abuses. The case that stands as the greatest warning of this potential is Rwanda: France had long provided security assistance to the Habyarimana regime in Rwanda, and elements of that regime were responsible for perpetrating the worst genocide since the Second World War—in part with weapons obtained from France and Belgium.[19] The

---

[14] George W. Grayson, "Los Zetas: The Ruthless Army Spawned by a Mexican Drug Cartel," Foreign Policy Research Institute E-Note, May 2008.

[15] Oeindrila Dube and Suresh Naidu, *Bases, Bullets, and Ballots: The Effect of U.S. Military Aid on Political Conflict in Colombia*, CGD Working Paper 197, Washington, D.C.: Center for Global Development, January 2010.

[16] Russell D. Howard, "Global Terrorism and U.S. Counterterrorism Policy in West Africa," *West Africa and the U.S. War on Terror*, George Klay Kieh and Kelechi Kalu, eds., New York: Routledge, 2013, p. 82; John B. Alexander, *Africa: Irregular Warfare on the Dark Continent*, Joint Special Operations University Report 09-5, May 2009, pp. 36–37.

[17] Adam Nossiter, Eric Schmitt, and Mark Mazzetti, "French Strikes in Mali Supplant Caution of U.S.", *New York Times*, January 13, 2013.

[18] Alice Hills, "Trojan Horses? USAID, Counterterrorism, and Africa's Police," *Third World Quarterly*, Vol. 27, No. 4, 2006, pp. 629–643.

[19] Gerard Prunier, *The Rwanda Crisis*, New York: Columbia University Press, 1995.

fact that France had provided assistance to the regime does not mean that it was responsible for the genocide. Nonetheless, following the atrocities in Rwanda, French public opinion turned decisively against French support for regimes in sub-Saharan Africa, leading France to pull back from most of its commitments on the continent for nearly two decades.[20]

Obviously, other cases in which foreign donors can be accused of abetting abuses are nowhere near so extreme as the Rwandan genocide. Moreover, in many cases, foreign decisionmakers faced complex trade-offs when making the decisions that ultimately linked their governments to the abuses of partner nations. In the Democratic Republic of Congo (DRC), for instance, forces trained by the United States were later accused of perpetrating widespread rape and other abuses.[21] Yet the government of the DRC desperately needed trained, capable forces to combat the many militias that were themselves committing atrocities throughout the eastern part of the country. Had the United States *not* provided security sector assistance, it could just as easily have been accused of failing to provide critical assistance to prevent atrocities. Similarly, the United States has provided military support to the government of Uganda to assist its efforts to counter the depredations of the Lord's Resistance Army, yet Ugandan forces themselves have been complicit in "gender-based violence and the exploitation of minerals."[22]

Moral Hazard

Finally, numerous regional experts have noted that regimes have considerable incentive *not* to solve the issues that prompt the United States and other donors to provide security sector and other forms of assistance. Transnational terrorism is seldom high on the list of security threats confronting most African actors, who may value contin-

---

[20] Xavier Renou, "A New French Policy for Africa?" *Journal of Contemporary African Studies*, Vol. 20, No. 1, 2002, pp. 5–27.

[21] Craig Whitlock, "U.S.-Trained Congolese Troops Committed Rapes and Other Atrocities, U.N. Says," *Washington Post*, May 13, 2013.

[22] Andre Le Sage, "Countering the Lord's Resistance Army in Central Africa," Strategic Forum No. 270, Washington, D.C.: National Defense University, July 2011, p. 14.

ued flows of foreign assistance much more than they value resolving their terrorism problems. Consequently, they forgo actions that might reduce or eliminate the terrorist threats that motivate U.S. assistance.[23] Similarly, regimes may have little incentive to resolve conflicts decisively so long as they can leverage these conflicts to gain considerable foreign assistance.[24]

Potential Strategic Consequences for the United States

As discussed above, the United States has committed itself in a variety of policy documents to a broad concern for the stability of partner nations in Africa. Obviously, if U.S. security sector assistance is potentially destabilizing, this in itself is cause for concern. But the strategic implications of failed security sector assistance policies extend beyond the direct and immediate consequences in the partner nation.

Perhaps most obviously, the United States risks being "tarred by the brush" of partner governments who act abusively toward their own populations. Even if the abusive behavior would have happened in the absence of U.S. security sector assistance—indeed, even if there is no link whatsoever between U.S. aid and the partner regime's actions—the United States' international reputation can suffer.[25]

The United States' reputation in the partner nation can also suffer, potentially with long-lasting consequences. One study found that the United States typically experienced poor relations with the

---

[23] For a general statement of this problem, see Navin A. Bapat, "Transnational Terrorism, U.S. Military Aid, and the Incentive to Misrepresent," *Journal of Peace Research*, Vol. 48, No. 3, 2011, pp. 303–318. For an application to Africa specifically, see Clint Watts, Jacob Shapiro, and Vahid Brown, *Al-Qa'ida's (Mis)Adventures in the Horn of Africa*, West Point, NY: Combatting Terrorism Center, 2007.

[24] Denis M. Tull and Pierre Englebert, "Postconflict Reconstruction in Africa: Flawed Ideas About Failed States," *International Security*, Vol. 32, No. 4, 2008, pp. 106–139.

[25] See, for instance, Daniel L. Byman, "Friends Like These: Counterinsurgency and the War on Terrorism," *International Security*, Vol. 31, No. 2, Fall 2006, p. 111.

democratic successors of autocratic regimes to which the U.S. had provided assistance.[26]

Failures of security sector assistance can also have a negative impact on continued U.S. domestic support for such policies. As noted earlier, the Rwandan genocide led to a broad retrenchment in France's relations with sub-Saharan Africa. Similarly, abuses by Salvadoran government forces during the war in El Salvador in the 1980s led the U.S. Congress to slash funding to the San Salvador regime.[27] Now, with the United States having withdrawn from Iraq and in the midst of its drawdown from Afghanistan, U.S. administrations may get more critical scrutiny of their smaller-scale military activities from Congress, the media, and elsewhere.

Finally, failures of security sector assistance often have subtler implications for the United States' ability to execute assistance policies elsewhere. USAID, for instance, faced considerable restrictions on its support for foreign police services after its support for abusive regimes in the 1960s and 1970s.[28] Problematic behavior by partner regimes also served as the inspiration for the so-called Leahy Law, which prohibits the provision of military assistance to units with a history of gross human rights violations. Many U.S. government officials complain about Leahy and similar restrictions—not because they disagree with the basic purpose of these provisions, but because they claim that the legislation is too inflexible and/or difficult to implement in practice. Yet the surest way of heading off such legislation in the future is to make appropriate investments in more flexible risk identification and

---

[26] Ely Ratner, "Reaping What You Sow: Democratic Transitions and Foreign Policy Realignment," *Journal of Conflict Resolution*, Vol. 53, No. 3, June 2009, pp. 390–418.

[27] Mark Peceny, "Two Paths to the Promotion of Democracy During U.S. Military Interventions," *International Studies Quarterly*, Vol. 39, No. 3, September 1995, pp. 371–401.

[28] David H. Bayley and Robert M. Perito, *The Police in War: Fighting Insurgency, Terrorism, and Violent Crime*, Boulder, Colo.: Lynne Rienner, 2010. For overviews of USAID guidance on support for foreign police, see U.S. Agency for International Development, *Assistance for Civilian Policing: USAID Policy Guidance*, PD-ACG-022, Washington, D.C., December 2005, particularly pp. 3–4; and U.S. Agency for International Development, *A Field Guide for USAID Democracy and Governance Officers: Assistance to Civilian Law Enforcement in Developing Countries*, Washington, D.C., January 2011.

mitigation strategies, before future abuses lead to even more restrictive legislation.

This chapter has focused on the risks of security sector assistance to fragile states. This focus is not meant to imply that the risks outweigh the benefits. Indeed, as some of the quantitative studies reviewed suggest, there is reason to believe that security sector assistance policies on balance play a positive role. They are most likely to go awry, however, in precisely the sorts of countries that lie at the center of U.S. terrorism concerns in Africa. Moreover, the various pathways by which security sector assistance can have destabilizing effects are not always straightforward or obvious even to experienced observers. It is for these reasons that these risks have been detailed at such length here, and it is for these reasons that U.S. interagency processes should systematically assess and plan for mitigating these risks.

CHAPTER THREE

Improving U.S. Security Sector Assistance Processes to Mitigate Risk

U.S. processes for planning, executing, and evaluating security sector assistance are undergoing significant change, which makes them a moving target for any analysis attempting to critique them and offer suggestions for their improvement. The recently released PPD 23 on Security Sector Assistance has launched important reforms, particularly in the areas of interagency coordination, planning, evaluation, resourcing, and oversight. Moreover, many U.S. personnel are deeply concerned about ensuring that U.S. security sector assistance has positive strategic effects, and they have undertaken a variety of initiatives at all levels to improve the performance of U.S. security sector assistance. Making generalizations about such a complex and rapidly evolving system is difficult. Nonetheless, at the time of this report's writing, the U.S. government lacked a systematic process for identifying and mitigating risks associated with security sector assistance to fragile states in the USAFRICOM area of responsibility.

Historically, the United States government has had procedures in place—such as End-Use Monitoring of security assistance—to terminate U.S. assistance if certain conditions are not met.[1] But when it

---

[1] The Defense Security Cooperation Agency explains End-Use Monitoring as follows:

> End-Use Monitoring (EUM) is a program designed to verify that defense articles or services transferred by the United States Government (USG) to foreign recipients are being used in accordance with the terms and conditions of the transfer agreement or other applicable agreement. In accordance with the Foreign Assistance Act (FAA), section 505, and the Arms Export Control Act (AECA), section 3 (22 U.S.C. 2753) and section 4 (22 U.S.C. 2754), as reflected in the Letter of Offer and Acceptance (LOA) Standard Terms and Conditions, recipients must agree to use U.S.-provided defense

comes to anticipating risks and mitigating them ahead of time, U.S. government procedures have been highly incomplete, driven more by intuitive and impressionistic judgments than by any rigorous and institutionalized process.

Moving forward, PPD 23—the current overarching guidance for U.S. security-sector assistance—seeks to build sustainable capacity through comprehensive sector strategies and to ensure that short-term interventions are consistent with long-term goals. It also emphasizes both improved oversight over SSA and improved monitoring and evaluation of SSA, including the development of "notional triggers" that would prompt the United States to reconsider its security sector assistance if any of these conditions come to pass.[2] This guidance represents significant progress for the U.S. SSA planning process. It continues, however, to put in place procedures that deal with risk primarily retroactively.

When asked about how they identify and mitigate risks in planning security sector assistance, many DoD planners emphasize that the State Department is intimately involved in even DoD-executed security sector assistance, all the way from the level of country teams at embassies throughout the world to planning processes in Washington,

---

articles, training, and services only for their intended purpose; not to transfer title to, or possession of, any defense article or related training to anyone not an officer, employee, or agent of that country or of the USG without prior written consent of the USG; to maintain the security of any article with substantially the same degree of protection afforded to it by the USG; and to permit observation and review by, and to furnish necessary information to, representatives of the USG with regards to use of such articles. EUM provides USG oversight to ensure these conditions are met. All potential end-use violations must be reported through Department of State (DoS) channels. Information regarding any potential violations should also be forwarded to the Golden Sentry program team at DSCA (Strategy Directorate, Weapons Division), the appropriate Combatant Commander (CCDR), and the Military Department (MILDEP).

(Defense Security Cooperation Agency, *Security Assistance Management Manual*, paragraph C8.1.1).

[2] A description of the PPD and guidance on its implementation is available in the document "Implementation of Security Sector Assistance (SSA) Presidential Policy Directive (PPD)" (undated).

D.C.[3] DoD planners do not themselves, however, have formal processes designed to identify risks ahead of time and take steps to mitigate them. State Department personnel are highly sensitive to the potential political risks of such assistance, but they typically think about risk identification and mitigation in highly informal, intuitive ways—ways that at least some at the State Department contend are inadequate to the many challenges posed by SSA.[4] Moreover, the State Department does not have adequate resources to oversee its current commitments, much less an expanded approach to risk identification and mitigation.[5] Neither DoD nor the State Department, in other words, appears well positioned to identify and mitigate SSA risks.

This chapter offers four recommendations for improving the United States' ability to anticipate and plan for such risks. As numerous studies have pointed out, the chief impediments to improved U.S. security sector assistance policies are ones that require congressional action—including a rationalization of the highly fractured legal authorities necessary to provide such assistance, a lengthening of the

---

[3] Anonymous interviews with over two dozen DoD personnel conducted at USAFRICOM in Stuttgart, Germany, November 2013; U.S. Army Africa (USARAF) in Vicenza, Italy, November 2013; and Combined Joint Task Force—Horn of Africa (CJTF-HOA) in Djibouti, July 2013.

[4] Anonymous interviews with nine State Department and USAID personnel responsible for security sector assistance planning, both global and specific to Africa, Washington, D.C., June–July 2013.

[5] The State Department has too few personnel, those personnel they do have often do not have expertise in military and security affairs, and their embassy personnel in Africa are often restricted by numbers and security restrictions from directly observing events outside of national capitals and other major cities. Beyond these resource constraints, some observers contend that the State Department also often suffers from limited political capital in disputes with other departments, particularly DoD. See, for instance, Robert B. Oakley and Michael Casey, *The Country Team: Restructuring America's First Line of Engagement*, Washington, D.C.: National Defense University, 2007; Cindy Williams and Gordon Adams, *Strengthening Statecraft and Security: Reforming U.S. Planning and Resource Allocation*, Cambridge, Mass.: MIT Security Studies Program, 2008, Chapter 4; Nina M. Serafino, Catherine Dale, and Pat Towell, *Building Civilian Interagency Capacity for Missions Abroad: Key Proposals and Issues for Congress,* Washington, D.C.: Congressional Research Service, 2012; Richard G. Lugar, *Embassies Grapple to Guide Foreign Aid: A Report to Members of the Committee on Foreign Relations*, Senate Foreign Relations Committee, United States Senate, S. Rpt. 110–33, 2007.

time frames over which budget allocations are made, and a re-balancing of resources to the benefit of civilian sectors.[6] Because these points have been made so thoroughly and convincingly elsewhere, this report will not repeat them. Rather, it offers less sweeping but more easily implementable recommendations—ones that the Departments of Defense and State can undertake without any changes to the legal or fiscal structure within which U.S. security sector assistance currently operates.

Recommendation 1: Develop Common "Theories" of Security Sector Assistance

Various official reports have lamented the inadequacies of U.S. security sector assistance planning processes and monitoring and evaluation (M&E) efforts.[7] Before rigorous interagency planning or monitoring and evaluation can occur, however, the government requires "theories of change" that specify what changes the United States expects to see as a result of its assistance and why. "Theories of change" or "logical frameworks" are government statements, somewhat analogous to military doctrine, about the expected results of given policies or programs. They are widely used in the development community and typi-

---

[6]   U.S. Department of State, Bureau of Arms Control, Verification, Compliance, International Security Advisory Board, *Report on Security Capacity Building*, Washington, D.C., 2013; Stewart Patrick, James Schear, and Mark Wong, *Integrating 21st Century Development and Security Assistance*, Final Report of the Task Force on Nontraditional Security Assistance, Washington, D.C.: Center for Strategic and International Studies, 2008; Williams and Adams, 2008, chapter 4; Bruce Estok, Heyward Hutson, Ken Saunders, and Tim Watson, "Trainers, Guns, and Money: Evolution or Revolution of Global Train and Equip," Cambridge, Mass.: Harvard Kennedy School; and Jennifer D. P. Moroney, David E. Thaler, and Joe Hogler, *Review of Security Cooperation Mechanisms Combatant Commands Utilize to Build Partner Capacity*, Santa Monica, Calif.: RAND Corporation, RR-413-OSD, 2013.

[7]   See, for instance, Government Accountability Office, "DoD and State Need to Improve Sustainment Planning and Monitoring and Evaluation for Section 1206 and 1207 Assistance Programs," GAO-10-431, Washington, D.C.: GAO, April 15, 2010; U.S. Department of Defense and U.S. Department of State, Inspectors General, *Interagency Evaluation of the Section 1206 Global Train and Equip Program*, Department of Defense Report No. IE-2009-007 and Department of State Report No. ISP-I-09-69, Washington, D.C., August 31, 2009.

cally developed in substantial part on the basis of empirical research conducted by academic or other researchers using rigorous analytic methods. Without such theories, it is simply impossible to know what exactly should be measured and how in any monitoring and evaluation effort, nor is it possible to account adequately for second- and third-order consequences in planning processes.[8] Currently the U.S. government lacks such "theories of change" for its security sector assistance—although efforts are reportedly under way to develop one.[9]

The U.S. Army has a highly elaborated "theory" of how to win conventional wars through the integrated use of fire and maneuver. It developed a similarly elaborate theory of counterinsurgency when faced with the wars in Iraq and Afghanistan. The Army, for instance, spent the first 30 pages of its revised doctrinal manual on counterinsurgency grappling with the theory and history of its subject. In the words of one of the field manual's authors, the introductory text was intended to "communicate that the standard manner of proceeding used by the general-purpose army must change in order to operate in a changed

---

[8] One expert defines a "theory of change" as follows:

> At its most basic, a theory of change explains how a group of early and intermediate accomplishments sets the stage for producing long-range results. A more complete theory of change articulates the assumptions about the process through which change will occur, and specifies the ways in which all of the required early and intermediate outcomes related to achieving the desired long-term change will be brought about and documented as they occur.

(Andrea Anderson, *The Community Builder's Approach to Theory of Change: A Practical Guide to Theory and Development*, New York: The Aspen Institute Roundtable on Community Change, 2005, p. 1).

For a review of "theories of change" in the development community, see Isabel Vogel, *Review of the Use of "Theory of Change" in International Development*, London: UK Department for International Development, 2012.

[9] Anonymous interview with USAID official, Washington, D.C., July 2013. See also Nicholas J. Armstrong, "The Prospects of Institutional Transfer: A Within-Case Study of NATO Advisor Influence Across the Afghan Security Ministries and National Security Forces, 2009–2012," a dissertation submitted at Maxwell School of Citizenship and Public Affairs, Syracuse University, May 2014.

world. . . . [T]he manual is an implicit call for the army to engage in an enthusiastic round of 'creative destruction.'"[10]

No similarly elaborate theory or call for "creative destruction" can be found in any of the Army's main doctrinal publications on security sector assistance, despite the fact that such assistance presents just as many challenges to standard U.S. Army practices as counterinsurgency does. The Army's field manual on security cooperation, for instance, is primarily concerned with U.S. bureaucratic processes.[11] It devotes only a couple of pages of sustained discussion to political, economic, and social considerations (other than cross-cultural communication).[12] The Army's "Army Security Cooperation Handbook" is even more focused on bureaucratic processes, with hardly any discussion of the partner-nation context.[13] Similarly, the U.S. Army Training and Doctrine Command's 40-page pamphlet, "The U.S. Army Concept for Building Partner Capacity," devotes only two extremely general paragraphs to the political considerations involved in supporting State Department security sector assistance programs.[14]

Nor is the Army the exception within DoD. A handbook on security cooperation recently released by the Office of the Secretary of Defense, for instance, frames security cooperation planning in terms of a typical "gap analysis," in which the planner determines what resources are required to eliminate the "gap" between the desired end state and current conditions. Nowhere in this "gap analysis" is there any men-

---

[10] See Douglass A. Ollivant's contributions to "'The New U.S. Army/Marine Corps Counterinsurgency Field Manual as Political Science and Political Praxis," *Perspectives on Politics,* Vol. 6, No. 2, June 2008, p. 357.

[11] Headquarters, U.S. Department of the Army, Field Manual (FM) 3-22, *Army Support to Security Cooperation,* January 2013.

[12] FM 3-22, pp. 3-5 and 3-6. It devotes another eight pages to "Considerations for Working Effectively with Foreign Security Forces" (Chapter 6), although almost the entire discussion focuses on inter-cultural communication, cultural sensitivity, and individual skills needed for teaching and mentoring.

[13] Headquarters, U.S. Department of the Army, *Army Security Cooperation Handbook,* Pamphlet 11-31, Washington, D.C., March 5, 2013.

[14] U.S. Army Training and Doctrine Command, *The U.S. Army Concept for Building Partner Capacity,* Pamphlet 525-8-4, November 22, 2011, pp. 21 and 24.

tion of the partner nation's ability or willingness to eliminate the "gap" that U.S. planners identify.[15] OSD and other institutions have been working to address these shortcomings. OSD's Security Cooperation Reform Task Force, for instance, addressed issues of partner ability and will. A number of publications from the Joint Center for International Security Force Assistance in Fort Leavenworth, Kansas, provide better discussions of the political, economic, and social contexts of SSA, although they remain far short of what they could or should be, and these discussions have not yet been incorporated into overarching guidance throughout DoD.[16]

In actual practice, many DoD planners, intelligence officers, and regional affairs officers spend considerable time focusing on partner nations' ability and willingness to build capabilities and enact reforms. But the lack of any kind of "theory of change" in the Army's or DoD's primary guidance documents suggests that such efforts are likely to be uncoordinated, ad hoc, incomplete, and subject to frequent change based on the personalities and backgrounds of the people occupying key positions. Contrast this situation with that in the United Kingdom's Department for International Development, which adopted a high-level focus on explicit "Drivers of Change" because the department believed that "Donors are good at identifying *what* needs to be done . . . [but] they are not always clear how to make this happen most effectively."[17] Similarly, the World Bank's "Logical Framework"—adapted from a process initially pioneered by USAID—"is used to develop the overall design of a project, to improve project implementation monitoring, and to strengthen periodic project evaluation. In essence, it is a 'cause & effect' model of project interventions to create desired impacts."[18]

---

[15] Office of the Deputy Assistant Secretary of Defense for Plans, *Theater Campaign Planning Planner's Handbook*, version 1.0, February 2012, pp. 15–16.

[16] See, for instance, Joint Center for International Security Force Assistance, *Commander's Handbook for Security Force Assistance*, Fort Leavenworth, Kan., July 14, 2008.

[17] UK Department for International Development, "Drivers of Change," November 2003.

[18] World Bank, *The Logframe Handbook: A Logical Framework Approach to Project Cycle Management*, Washington, D.C., 2005.

As DoD increasingly orients itself toward "shaping" operations and "wars among the people," it needs to build a corresponding sophistication. Currently, the closest thing to an official U.S. "theory of change" or "logical framework" specifically designed for the security sector can be found in the interagency statement on security sector reform, which discusses how a variety of actors might demand greater accountability and effectiveness from state security providers if empowered through appropriate policies and practices.[19] This document appears to capture much of how USAID and the State Department think about security sector assistance.[20] But there are a number of problems with relying on it as the only statement of the "theory of change" underlying U.S. security sector assistance. Most importantly, as discussed above, security sector reform encompasses only some of the goals of U.S. security sector assistance. Moreover, the United States government is poorly structured to conduct SSR; DoD, for instance, lacks many of the authorities and capabilities it would need to better connect security forces with reformed governance and political structures. It is also not clear that security sector reform as currently conceived can be effectively used as a preventive tool outside of the contexts for which it was originally created—post-conflict and rapidly democratizing countries. It is in part for these reasons that DoD personnel interviewed for this report seldom embraced security sector reform as the overarching vision of what they were trying to support through DoD-led security cooperation activities. Although inadequate as an overarching framework for all U.S. security sector assistance, U.S. guidance on security sector reform does provide considerable material that could be incorporated into a broader framework for understanding how the United States might maximize the positive contributions of its assistance.

Ongoing efforts to develop Army and Joint doctrine for security cooperation offer opportunities to incorporate such risk-assessment and -mitigation frameworks into DoD guidance. DoD should also

---

[19] U.S. Agency for International Development, U.S. Department of Defense, and U.S. Department of State, *Security Sector Reform*, February 2009.

[20] Anonymous interviews with officials at USAID and the State Department, Washington, D.C., June–July 2013.

incorporate such frameworks into its Guidance for Employment of the Force (GEF), and DoD and the State Department should also include guidance along these lines in their country and regional strategies. The "theory of change" or "logical framework" should also shape the Measures of Performance and Measures of Effectiveness by which DoD evaluates its efforts.

Recommendation 2: Improve Risk Identification Through Formal Risk Assessment Frameworks and More Robust Data Collection

The systematic and documented identification and monitoring of risk is almost completely absent from official U.S. security sector assistance processes. This absence is noteworthy in light of the prevalence of program M&E and early warning systems for violent conflict among major donor governments (including the United States) and international organizations.[21]

There has been an increasing emphasis recently on monitoring and evaluation of such assistance, spurred in part by impending and anticipated budget cuts and in part by the trend toward such practices in the development community generally and USAID specifically.[22] In all monitoring and evaluation products reviewed or discussed with relevant offices in the course of this study, however, inadvertent negative outcomes were never the subject of U.S. government data collection

---

[21] For a review of early warning systems, see Organisation for Economic Co-operation and Development, *Preventing Violence, War and State Collapse: The Future of Conflict Early Warning and Response*, Paris: OECD, 2009.

[22] PPD 23 emphasizes improved monitoring and evaluation. Unfortunately, U.S. efforts to evaluate the effectiveness of its security sector assistance began at such a low baseline that there is nowhere to go but up. The lack of systematic evaluation has been a continuing refrain in GAO and other reports on U.S. security sector assistance. See, for instance, GAO, 2010; Department of Defense and Department of State Inspectors General, 2009; Jennifer D. P. Moroney, Beth Grill, Joe L. Hogler, Lianne Kennedy-Boudali, and Christopher Paul, *How Successful Are U.S. Efforts to Build Capacity in Developing Countries?: A Framework to Assess the Global Train and Equip "1206" Program*, Santa Monica, Calif.: RAND Corporation, TR-1121-OSD, 2011.

efforts; evaluation efforts sought only to identify the extent of positive achievements of U.S. security sector assistance.[23] Such M&E initiatives are necessary and a positive indication of relevant agencies' increasing dedication to rigorous analysis of programming effectiveness. Given the risks of security sector assistance in fragile states detailed in the previous section, however, these initiatives are not adequate.

The informal, intuitive approach to risk identification and monitoring generally adopted by the State Department is insufficient to this task. It is important to note that a wide range of development actors have found such approaches highly problematic, particularly in the context of fragile states, and have instead adopted formal assessment procedures. In one recent guidance note, the United Nations Development program observed, "Many Country Office staff use their knowledge of the context somewhat intuitively for programming—but often, they have only a partial view of the context in question. Consequently, many projects fail."[24] Similarly, in the introduction to its Conflict Assessment Framework, USAID declared,

> The importance of a tool that facilitates dispassionate and objective analysis of conflict cannot be overstated. . . .To avoid unwanted negative outcomes from assistance, such as inadvertently supporting one side against the other, it is essential for international actors to develop an independent, objective view of the conflict. A conflict assessment is a tool to facilitate this process. To be successful, therefore, assessment teams and those who work with them should adopt sound procedures and structures to uphold intellectual honesty and integrity throughout the process, to maintain transparency in the methodology, and to protect sensitive information when it is disclosed . . . [I]t is also imperative

---

[23] Anonymous interviews with officials at USAID and the State Department, Washington, D.C., June–July 2013; USAFRICOM in Stuttgart, Germany, November 2013; USARAF in Vicenza, Italy, November 2013; and Combined Joint Task Force—Horn of Africa (CJTF-HOA) in Djibouti, July 2013.

[24] United Nations Development Program (UNDP), "Institutional and Context Analysis Guidance Note," New York, 2012, p. 4.

to actively seek information from diverse stakeholders in a given context.[25]

The World Bank reached a similar conclusion:

At a minimum, donors need to ensure that they respect the "Do No Harm" principle and that their interventions are attuned to the specific risks of state fragility. A more consistent consideration of [context] can also help to move from working "in" fragility and conflict to working "on" (overcoming) fragility and conflict. The premise of this note is that the donor community can do better in identifying the priorities, sequencing, and trade-offs which are inevitably involved.[26]

The OECD Development Assistance Community had an even more negative assessment of the consequences of relying on intuitive understandings of programs' local context:

Donor communities have great difficulty coming to terms with the overlay of politics, power relationships and incentive structures that affect the governance and accountability contexts within which their development co-operation approaches and instruments must function and achieve results. This has led to programming assumptions which can be far removed from the power dynamics and political realities on the ground, or which cannot adequately address the interaction between formal and informal political, economic and social processes. Too often donors apply approaches, models and instruments that have been used in their own countries to developing country actors and institutions—but often these are not suited to the local contexts and challenges.[27]

---

[25] USAID, *Conflict Assessment Framework*, Version 2.0, June 2012.

[26] World Bank Public Sector and Governance Group, "Guidance for Supporting State-Building in Fragile and Conflict-Affected States: A Tool-Kit," Washington, D.C., July 12, 2012, p. 9.

[27] Organisation for Economic Co-operation and Development Development Assistance Committee, *Accountability and Democratic Governance: Orientations and Principles for Development*, Paris, 2013, p. 17.

Finally, in a section of its "Drivers of Change" paper ("What Difference Will This Make?") the United Kingdom's Department for International Development noted several specific outcomes that it expected to materialize as a result of its more systematic approach to analyzing local context:

- Develop more focused and strategic plans to influence the underlying structural and institutional determinants of the desired end state
- "Develop more realistic timeframes and indicators"
- "Unpack the notion of 'lack of political will' where this is identified as a major risk to program success"
- Identify policies and programs that may not directly achieve the outcomes of interest but that have positive indirect effects
- "Think seriously about how aid affects incentives, and about donors as political actors."[28]

Such a structured approach to contextual and risk analysis should resonate with military planners. U.S. military doctrine is filled with requirements to anticipate how adversaries may react in unexpected ways (e.g., through "red-teaming") and to develop plans with branches and sequels in order to prepare for risk.[29] Obviously, partner nations are not adversaries, but they do frequently react in unanticipated ways to U.S. initiatives, and their independent agendas do imply risks to U.S. interests. It is therefore unclear why DoD planners would not invest in systematic risk analysis as a part of its efforts—alongside those of other agencies of the U.S. government—to conduct security sector assistance planning.

Existing U.S. government tools could serve as the initial basis for elaborating formal risk assessment frameworks. The U.S. guidance on security sector reform provides many elements of such a framework.

---

[28] DFID, 2003, p. 3.

[29] See, for instance, U.S. Joint Chiefs of Staff, Joint Publication 2-0, *Joint Intelligence*, October 22, 2013; and U.S. Joint Chiefs of Staff, Joint Publication 5-0, *Joint Operation Planning*, August 11, 2011.

USAID's Conflict Assessment Framework, intended for use globally, and its District Stability Framework, created for use in Afghanistan, both provide useful overarching frameworks for understanding conflict dynamics.[30]

Both U.S. SSR guidance and its conflict assessment guidance, however, need to be elaborated and adapted specifically to the risks posed by security sector assistance in fragile states. The United States' SSR policy does not provide a sufficient basis for less intensive and comprehensive forms of security cooperation, while the conflict assessment tools that USAID has developed focus particularly on inter-communal conflict and not on other forms of political risk (such as rent-seeking, the creation of "praetorian guards," and so on) discussed previously. The possible risks of security sector assistance outlined in the previous section of this report are a step in this direction.

These political risk assessment frameworks should act as a guide to help U.S. planners and implementers understand the different types of actors with which the United States will have to act and what can reasonably be expected of each given their domestic constraints, the appropriate time frames for the United States' various goals, and the likely second- and third-order effects of U.S. security sector assistance. They will act as a bureaucratic "forcing function," requiring the various components of the U.S. government to undertake systematic conversations about the trade-offs inherent in security sector assistance and whether the anticipated gains are worth the risks of operating in fragile states. Finally, they should serve as a guide to more precise evaluation efforts in a handful of countries and issues of particular concern.

Unfortunately, DoD and the rest of the U.S. government currently lack the data they require to conduct systematic risk analysis. Much of the data that are supposed to be collected are highly

---

[30] USAID, 2012; and U.S. Agency for International Development, Office of Military Affairs, "District Stability Framework," presented at the Military Operations Research Society Mini-Symposium on Social Science Underpinnings of Complex Operations. Political economy analysis tools also represent a useful point of departure; see, for instance, UK Department for International Development, "Political Economy Analysis How To Note," London, July 2009; and Verena Fritz, Brian Levy, and Rachel Ort, *Problem-Driven Political Economy Analysis: The World Bank's Experience*, Washington, D.C.: World Bank, 2014.

incomplete—perhaps in part because many of these monitoring and evaluation frameworks are relatively new and not yet perceived as a routine responsibility, but perhaps also in part because these frameworks have not yet generated products perceived as useful by those who are responsible for inputting data. Those data that do exist are of variable quality. The same personnel responsible for implementing programs are typically conducting evaluations of those programs' effectiveness. At a minimum, such systems are subject to a perception that these personnel, either consciously or unconsciously, inflate their estimates of the programs' effectiveness.[31]

Even if the U.S. government were dedicated to rigorously assessing potential risks of security sector assistance in fragile states, it is important to acknowledge that it would encounter significant challenges to acquiring the necessary data. Many, if not most, governments, particularly among fragile states, are reluctant to allow foreign governments systematic access to their security forces—the sort of access that would be necessary to measure a military's skills acquisition and retention over time, to assess its ability to provide timely paychecks and reasonable facilities to its forces, or to conduct opinion polls among officers and soldiers. Similarly, many governments are reluctant to allow public opinion polling, particularly on sensitive matters such as inter-communal tensions or abuses by security services. Even more impressionistic data gathering may be difficult outside of the major cities in highly insecure countries. Moreover, all assessment efforts cost money, and they may not be justified—or perceived to be justified— particularly in countries that do not receive substantial amounts of U.S. assistance.

These limitations suggest that an optimal research design for risk assessment or program evaluation will seldom be possible. Partial solutions, however, are entirely feasible. At a minimum, the United States could work with willing partners who are significant recipients of U.S. assistance to implement more complete risk assessments and program evaluations. Such willing partners would almost certainly represent a biased sample—"best-case scenarios"—else they would likely be

---

[31] Moroney et al., 2011, p. 4.

unwilling to provide the United States broad access for data gathering. Such a sample could not be used to make generalizations about the effectiveness of security sector assistance among all partner nations. It might, however, at least provide rigorous data on the best-case partner nations. If security sector assistance shows few signs of building durable improvements in these best-case partners' capabilities, or if it leads to significant negative side-effects, then such evidence would suggest serious limits to the impact of U.S. security sector assistance. If, on the other hand, such partners experienced enduring improvements in their capabilities without experiencing negative second- or third-order effects, it would provide some of the most rigorous evidence to date of the potential for security sector assistance to make positive contributions in at least certain environments.

Working where possible with partner-nation government and civil society organizations may make many forms of data gathering feasible, particularly in cases where postcolonial resentments of donor nations run high. If partner-nation decisionmakers see evaluation processes as co-led by their own nationals, they are more likely to see these processes as a valuable opportunity rather than as a source of donor-nation criticism. Such partnerships are still unlikely among more autocratic regimes, but they may well be possible with more democratic partners.[32] Similarly, involving appropriate "peer mentors" from other developing countries may facilitate cooperation. In such cases of "South-South mentoring," developing countries are asked to second civil servants with appropriate skills to other developing countries— often ones emerging from conflict or other crisis—to act as advisors in their ministries.[33] Such advisors might help to catalyze evaluation processes, acting as facilitators between the donor and recipient nations.

---

[32] Involving partner nations in the evaluation of assistance has become a core principle of international development assistance generally and security sector reform specifically. See, for instance, the Organisation for Economic Co-operation and Development's *The Paris Declaration on Aid Effectiveness*, 2005, and its *Handbook on Security System Reform*, 2007, especially pp. 94–96.

[33] See, especially, United Nations, *Civilian Capacity in the Aftermath of Conflict: Independent Report of the Senior Advisory Group*, 2011; Kristoffer N. Tarp and Frederik F. Rosén, "Coaching and Mentoring for Capacity Development: The Case of South Sudan," *African*

Other mechanisms might be used to facilitate data gathering in insecure peripheral regions of conflict-affected countries. U.S. Army Civil Affairs Teams (CATs) have been used in such roles in several countries in Africa. Their success has largely been determined by their relationships with the U.S. ambassador; where the U.S. mission does not see value in their activities, they will inevitably fail.[34] With appropriate selection of personnel for the CATs and sufficient preliminary coordination with the ambassador and country team, CATs might be used effectively where other mechanisms are unavailable. Contractors—from either the United States or the partner nation—might also be utilized in this role (a point elaborated in Recommendation 4 below).

Improved cooperation across the U.S. government is critical both to financing improved risk-identification processes and to leveraging its findings. Assessment and evaluation of U.S. security sector assistance is currently distributed among a bewildering variety of actors. To a certain extent, this fragmentation is logical: Different bureaucratic actors have different roles in U.S. security sector assistance processes, and so they require information on different issues. But much of these assessment and evaluation efforts are duplicative. The result is a large number of overlapping products, each of which is underresourced, and the totality of which exceeds decisionmakers' ability to read and digest. Were the various bureaucratic entities involved in U.S. security sector assistance to pool their resources to undertake more systematic and robust assessment and evaluation efforts and to freely share the results of these efforts throughout the interagency, solid risk identification processes would become much more feasible.[35]

Security Review, Vol. 21, No. 1, March 2012, pp. 15–30; and Kristoffer N. Tarp and Frederik F. Rosén, "Building Civil Servant Capacity in South Sudan," Policy Brief, Copenhagen: Danish Institute for International Studies, October 2011.

[34] Anonymous interviews with personnel in CJTF-HOA, Djibouti, July 2013, and in USARAF, Vicenza, Italy, November 2013.

[35] At the time of writing, it was unclear what actions the SSA Oversight Board and the SSA Interagency Policy Committee would undertake with regard to the rationalization of assessment and evaluation processes.

Recommendation 3: Improve Planning to Enable Risk Mitigation

Despite being an organization that runs on extensive planning, DoD has placed remarkably little emphasis on planning for mitigating the risks of security sector assistance to fragile states.

What might such advance planning look like in practice?

There are at least four things the United States could do to improve planning for risk mitigation. First, the United States should move forward with plans to identify possible "triggers" that would indicate when decisionmakers should review security sector assistance for termination, as required by PPD 23.[36] These triggers might be included in the Integrated Country Strategies required by the directive. The United States should also act to ensure that the burden of proof is placed on those who would continue assistance despite warning signs in the partner nation. Too often both top decisionmakers and the working levels of bureaucracies become overly committed to the continuation of policies that are in place, even when there is considerable evidence that these policies are having counterproductive effects.[37]

Second, U.S. security sector assistance to high-risk countries should focus as much as possible on training and education activities. The review of the quantitative literature on security sector assistance above showed considerable consensus on the higher degree of risk associated with transfers of material assistance (e.g., FMF) than with programs focused on training and education (e.g., International Military Education and Training [IMET]). Of course, some governments insist on material assistance, either because they see little utility in U.S. training or because they resent many of the democratic or human rights

---

[36] The State Department was assigned the responsibility for developing such triggers in PPD-23.

[37] In military contexts, see, for instance, George W. Downs, "The Lessons of Disengagement," *Foreign Military Intervention: The Dynamics of Protracted Conflict,* Ariel E. Levite, Bruce W. Jentleson, and Larry Berman, eds., New York: Columbia University Press, 1992; in development contexts, see Nicolas van de Walle, *Overcoming Stagnation in Aid-Dependent Countries,* Washington, D.C.: Center for Global Development, 2005, especially chapters 3 and 4.

principles incorporated into U.S. programs.[38] Such reactions, however, might themselves be an indication of particularly high risk. A period of successful participation in training and education programs could be a precondition for significant material assistance—not necessarily because it prevents misdeeds and abuses in the future, but because it has the potential to provide information on the partner's commitment to security practices in line with U.S. requirements.

Third, the United States might create career incentive systems that reward long-term performance. Both the State Department and Department of Defense use personnel systems that frequently rotate individuals through assignments, some of which last for less than a year. Such personnel management practices tend to reward individuals for accomplishments visible within an individual's period of assignment—and, conversely, to devalue the long-term consequences (both positive and negative) of an individual's actions. It is not easy to develop an incentive system that distributes rewards (or censure) based on the performance of programs that unfold over multiple rotation cycles. To the extent such a system is feasible, however, it would clearly emphasize the importance of evaluating and mitigating the long-term risks of security sector assistance.

Recommendation 4: Improve Execution in Ways that Mitigate Risks

There are many ways in which the United States could improve the execution of its security sector assistance to mitigate its potential risks. The following possibilities are meant to be illustrative rather than exhaustive.

Improved Regional Expertise

Numerous publications have recommended developing greater regional awareness among the military personnel executing security cooperation

---

[38] See, for instance, Watts et al., 2014, chapter 5.

as a means to improve the effectiveness of such activities.[39] There are important trade-offs involved in such proposals. Substantially increasing the regional awareness of large numbers of U.S. military personnel would require significant investments in training and education, and the time devoted to these activities would be time that these personnel would be unable to spend on other activities, including training on military tasks or potentially remaining available for immediate deployment. On the other hand, there are costs associated with low levels of regional awareness. Many regional specialists in both the U.S. Army and the State Department who were interviewed in the course of this study expressed concerns about what they perceived as inadequate sensitivity to local political considerations among U.S. Army general purpose forces.[40] U.S. ambassadors and their country teams not infrequently place strict restrictions on the activities of U.S. military personnel for fear of their causing political problems in partner nations.[41]

To some extent, the U.S. Army and Department of Defense have addressed such criticisms. It is important to note that the military officers who head Security Cooperation Offices (SCOs) in Africa are either Foreign Area Officers or (typically in more austere or dangerous missions) Special Operations Forces, both of which have extensive education and experience in their regions. SCO personnel, however, help only to formulate security sector assistance plans. Actual implementation is typically conducted by personnel with considerably less regional expertise. One important initiative to address this deficit was the formation of Regionally Aligned Forces, which emphasize regional awareness in their training. Such training, however, lasts only a few days—

---

[39] See, for instance, Michael D. Jason, "Integrating the Advisory Effort in the Army: A Full-Spectrum Solution," *Military Review*, September–October 2008, pp. 27–32; John A. Nagl, "Institutionalizing Adaptation: It's Time for an Army Advisor Command," *Military Review*, September–October 2008, pp. 21–26; Scott G. Wuestner, *Building Partner Capacity/Security Force Assistance: A New Structural Paradigm,* Carlisle Barracks, Pa.: Strategic Studies Institute, U.S. Army War College, 2009.

[40] Anonymous interviews with U.S. diplomatic and military personnel, conducted in multiple locations from June to November 2013.

[41] Anonymous interviews with U.S. military personnel in Djibouti, July 2013.

enough to provide basic sensitivity to local context to forces deploying overseas, but little more.

There are numerous reforms that the U.S. Army could undertake to improve regional awareness among the personnel most critical for implementing partnership activities. One such possibility would be to extend the tour lengths of personnel serving in headquarters assignments. Longer tours would increase the level of regional familiarity that headquarters staff members bring to their work. This familiarity would improve the quality of security sector planning they conduct. These headquarters officers can also serve as liaison officers, temporarily deployed to Africa to provide additional regional expertise to general purpose forces conducting security cooperation activities.

A more far-reaching proposal would create a "habitual alignment" between individuals and one or two regions of the world. Commissioned officers would be aligned to one or two regions corresponding to the Geographic Combatant Commands upon commissioning (or potentially even earlier, at the outset of their military academy or ROTC education). They would be expected to take a certain number of elective courses in appropriate languages and area studies at each stage of their professional military education, they would be offered small bonuses and other incentives throughout their careers to attain and retain appropriate language proficiency, and their career assignments would be designed in such a way as to ensure some period of deployment time in the appropriate region or regions. A similar progression could be developed for noncommissioned officers. Such an approach is similar to one that the U.S. Marine Corps adopted, the Regional, Culture, and Language Familiarization (RCLF) Program.[42]

It is impractical to create high levels of regional familiarity among all military personnel who might be deployed for security cooperation activities. But the Army and DoD more generally should study these and other ways of improving the regional familiarity of critical staff whose expertise might serve as "multipliers" for the effectiveness of other general purpose forces. At a minimum, they should incorporate

---

[42] See "Implementation of the Regional, Culture, and Language Familiarization Program," Marines: The Official Website of the United States Marine Corps, October 24, 2012.

risk analysis as a component of regional expertise and security cooperation training.

Embedded Personnel

Embedding U.S. personnel—or potentially those of appropriate partners—in the security ministries of partner nations potentially offers numerous advantages for risk identification and mitigation. Embedded U.S. personnel are much better able to observe dynamics within partner-nation forces, allowing them to adapt U.S. security sector assistance or, in the extreme, recommend terminating it altogether. Embedded personnel also have the opportunity to establish relationships of trust with partner-nation leaders. At least in certain contexts, embedded mentors—either from the United States or from relatively capable, democratic, developing countries willing to second such personnel—have proven highly effective.[43] The U.S. Ministry of Defense Advisors (MoDA) program provides one mechanism for such embedded advisors. The program's scale, however, does not yet come close to matching the potential demand in Africa.

Use of Contractors

The United States should also assess how it uses contractors in security sector assistance. Interviews with personnel involved in security sector assistance suggest radically different perceptions of both the quality and usage of contractors. Some interviewees suggested that contractors possessed skills, experience, and relationships superior to those of U.S. uniformed personnel, most of whom cycle rapidly through different positions. These same interviewees suggested that the State Department was able to work extremely effectively with contractors, establishing long-term relationships based on trust and high levels of information sharing. Other interviewees pointed to very different examples: contractors who had not been well vetted and lacked the necessary

---

[43] See, for instance, Watts et al., 2014, chapter 4; and Tarp and Rosén, 2011 and 2012. See also the brief discussion of foreign advisors paired with the broader discussion of local knowledge and oversight in Joseph H. Felter, "Taking Guns to a Knife Fight: Effective Military Support to Counterinsurgency," unpublished manuscript, West Point, N.Y.: U.S. Military Academy, February 16, 2007.

skills or attributes for their positions, contractors who abided by a very narrow interpretation of their contracts that did not permit them to share information freely with U.S. government personnel, and contractors who lacked appropriate relationships with U.S. embassy personnel, ensuring that the contractors' work would be divorced from the broader political goals being pursued by the United States.[44]

It is likely that these perspectives all represent different pieces of the broader picture—that the United States' experience with contractors, in other words, is highly variable depending on the personalities involved, the specifics of the contract, and the local context. Certainly the best contractors have the *potential* to offer skills and regional experience beyond that of most uniformed personnel. Realizing contractors' potential, however, requires careful vetting, appropriately designed contracts, robust contract oversight, and considerable effort to establish strong relationships with the relevant U.S. embassy or embassies. At a minimum, the United States government should ensure that contracts include broad information-sharing requirements; otherwise, the information that contractors obtain in the course of their interactions with partner-nation personnel will not become part of the broader U.S. effort to identify and track risks associated with security sector assistance. To the extent possible, U.S. embassies should work to establish regular channels of communication with contractors and make the renewal of contracts dependent on contractors' integration into more politically relevant, risk-attuned concepts of security sector assistance.

These recommendations are intended as only a jumping-off point to a broader discussion about incorporating a greater awareness of risks into the implementation of U.S. assistance policies. A much-expanded list is both possible and indeed imperative if the United States is to adopt risk mitigation policies in security sector assistance as it does in other fields.

---

[44] Anonymous interviews with U.S. and foreign personnel in Djibouti, July 2013; at the Department of State, July 2013; and with contractors by telephone, July 2009.

CHAPTER FOUR
Conclusion

This report has focused on documenting the risks that security sector assistance poses to the fragile states of Africa: their extent, the specific mechanisms by which they operate, the reasons for these risks, the manner in which the U.S. government currently deals with these risks, and ways in which the United States could do better. Most such risks are relatively small scale: They may be a relatively minor contributing factor to long-standing inter-communal tensions, or they may weaken governance institutions that were already severely flawed. But the potential exists for more serious failures that may reverberate in ways that do long-lasting damage to U.S. foreign policy.

The focus on risk is not meant to imply that the negative second- and third-order consequences are the predominant outcomes. Indeed, the quantitative evidence reviewed in this report provides reason to believe that security sector assistance is, on balance, a stabilizing influence. The report's focus was instead motivated by a desire to improve the functioning of such assistance and to avoid having one or more high-profile failures in the future cause the United States to pull back from all such efforts.

U.S. military planning emphasizes risk assessment and contingency planning. Similarly, the development community has put in place many systematic frameworks for assessing partner-nation political structures and the potential for foreign assistance to inflame conflict in fragile states.[1] Both the military and development communities

---

[1] See, for instance, United Nations Development Programme, Bureau for Crisis Prevention and Recovery, *Conflict-Related Development Analysis (CDA)*, October 2003; Organisation for

in recent years have placed much greater emphasis on program monitoring and evaluation. Yet despite these trends, formal risk assessment and planning for their mitigation is almost entirely absent from U.S. security sector assistance processes. This report suggests that the continued absence of such procedures—most of which are already at hand and relatively easy to implement—jeopardizes U.S. efforts to achieve its goals in Africa and beyond, potentially at significant cost to U.S. interests. Adopting risk assessment and mitigation practices will certainly not eliminate the risks of cooperating with fragile regimes, but they offer a low-cost means of managing those risks while still pursuing critical U.S. goals.

Economic Co-operation and Development Development Assistance Committee, *Supporting Statebuilding in Situations of Conflict and Fragility*, Paris, 2011; UNDP, 2012; USAID, 2012.

References

Alexander, John B., *Africa: Irregular Warfare on the Dark Continent*, Joint Special Operations University Report 09-5, May 2009, pp. 36–37.

Anderson, Andrea A., *The Community Builder's Approach to Theory of Change: A Practical Guide to Theory and Development*, New York: Aspen Institute Roundtable on Community Change, 2005.

Atkinson, Carol, "Constructivist Implications of Material Power: Military Engagement and the Socialization of States, 1972–2000," *International Studies Quarterly*, Vol. 50, No. 3, September 2006, pp. 509–537.

Bachmann, Jan, and Jana Hönke, "'Peace and Security' as Counterterrorism? The Political Effects of Liberal Interventions in Kenya," *African Affairs*, Vol. 109, No. 434, 2009, pp. 97–114.

Ball, Nicole, *Promoting Security Sector Reform in Fragile States,* PPC Issue Paper No. 11, Washington, D.C.: U.S. Agency for International Development, April 2005.

Ball, Nicole, Piet Biesheuvel, Tom Hamilton-Baillie, and 'Funmi Olonisakin, *Security and Justice Sector Reform Programming in Africa*, Evaluation Working Paper 23, London, UK: Department for International Development, April 2007.

Bapat, Navin A., "Transnational Terrorism, U.S. Military Aid, and the Incentive to Misrepresent," *Journal of Peace Research*, Vol. 48, No. 3, May 2011, pp. 303–318.

Bayley, David H., and Robert M. Perito, *The Police in War: Fighting Insurgency, Terrorism, and Violent Crime*, Boulder, Colo.: Lynne Rienner, 2010.

Bendix, Daniel, and Ruth Stanley, "Security Sector Reform in Africa: The Promise and the Practice of a New Donor Approach," Durban, South Africa: ACCORD Occasional Paper Series, Vol. 3, No. 2, 2008.

Berschinski, Robert G., *AFRICOM's Dilemma: The "Global War on Terrorism," "Capacity Building," Humanitarianism, and the Future of U.S. Security Policy in Africa*, Carlisle Barracks, Pa.: Strategic Studies Institute, U.S. Army War College, 2007.

Blanton, Shannon Lindsey, "Instruments of Security or Tools of Repression? Arms Imports and Human Rights Conditions in Developing Countries," *Journal of Peace Research*, Vol. 36, No. 2, 1999, pp. 233–244.

Bonnemaison, Eric, "Security Sector Planning in Africa: Military Force as a Public Good," *African Security Review*, Vol. 11, No. 2, 2002.

Bräutigam, Deborah, *Aid Dependence and Governance*, Stockholm: Expert Group on Development Issues, 2000.

Bryden, Matt, *Somalia Redux? Assessing the New Somali Federal Government*, Lanham, Md.: Center for Strategic and International Studies, Rowman and Littlefield, August 2013.

Byman, Daniel L., "Friends Like These: Counterinsurgency and the War on Terrorism," *International Security*, Vol. 31, No. 2, Fall 2006, pp. 79–115.

Defense Security Cooperation Agency, *Security Assistance Management Manual*, chapt. 8. As of October 3, 2014:
http://www.samm.dsca.mil/chapter/chapter-8

Downs, George W., "The Lessons of Disengagement," in Ariel E. Levite, Bruce W. Jentleson, and Larry Berman, eds., *Foreign Military Intervention: The Dynamics of Protracted Conflict*, New York: Columbia University Press, 1992.

Dube, Oeindrila, and Suresh Naidu, *Bases, Bullets, and Ballots: The Effect of U.S. Military Aid on Political Conflict in Colombia*, CGD Working Paper 197, Washington, D.C.: Center for Global Development, January 2010.

Ellis, Stephen, "Briefing: The Pan-Sahel Initiative," *African Affairs*, Vol. 103, No. 412, 2004, pp. 459–464.

Feyzioglu, Tarhan, Vinaya Swaroop, and Min Zhu, "A Panel Data Analysis of the Fungibility of Foreign Aid," *World Bank Economic Review*, Vol. 12, No. 1, 1998, pp. 29–58.

Fisher, Jonathan, "Managing Donor Perceptions: Contextualizing Uganda's 2007 Intervention in Somalia," *African Affairs*, Vol. 111, No. 444, 2012, pp. 404–423.

Fitch, John Samuel, "The Political Impact of U.S. Military Aid to Latin America: Institutional and Individual Effects," *Armed Forces and Society*, Vol. 5, 1979, pp. 360–386.

Fritz, Verena, Brian Levy, and Rachel Ort, *Problem-Driven Political Economy Analysis: The World Bank's Experience*, Washington, D.C.: World Bank, 2014

Fund for Peace, Failed States Index 2013, web page, 2013. As of October 2, 2014:
http://ffp.statesindex.org/rankings-2013-sortable

Global Facilitation Network for Security Sector Reform, *A Beginner's Guide to Security Sector Reform (SSR)*, December 2007.

Grayson, George W., "Los Zetas: The Ruthless Army Spawned by a Mexican Drug Cartel," Foreign Policy Research Institute E-Note, May 2008. As of October 3, 2014:
http://www.fpri.org/enotes/200805.grayson.loszetas.html

Gutelius, David, "Islam in Northern Mali and the War on Terror," *Journal of Contemporary African Studies*, Vol. 25, No. 1, 2007, pp. 59–76.

Ham, General Carter, U.S. Army Commander, U.S. Africa Command, statement before the U.S. House Armed Services Committee, March 1, 2012.

Headquarters, U.S. Department of the Army, *Army Support to Security Cooperation*, FM 3-22, January 2013.

———, *Army Security Cooperation Handbook*, Pamphlet 11-31, Washington, D.C., March 5, 2013.

Herbst, Jeffrey, "African Militaries and Rebellion: The Political Economy of Threat and Combat Effectiveness," *Journal of Peace Research*, Vol. 41, No. 3, May 2004, pp. 357–369.

High-Level Forum on African Perspectives on SSR and Experts-Level Seminar on African Perspectives on SSR, *African Perspectives on Security Sector Reform*, United Nations Department of Peacekeeping Operations, Office of Rule of Law and Security Institutions Security Sector Reform Unit, May 14, 2010.

Hills, Alice, "Trojan Horses? USAID, Counterterrorism and Africa's Police," *Third World Quarterly*, Vol. 27, No. 4, 2006, pp. 629–643.

Howard, Russell D., "Global Terrorism and U.S. Counterterrorism Policy in West Africa," in George Klay Kieh and Kelechi Kalu, eds., *West Africa and the U.S. War on Terror*, New York: Routledge, 2013.

Howe, Herbert M., *Ambiguous Order: Military Forces in African States*, Boulder, Colo.: Lynne Rienner, 2001.

International Dialogue on Peacebuilding and Statebuilding, *The Monrovia Roadmap on Peacebuilding and Statebuilding*, July 2011. As of October 2, 2014:
http://www.pbsbdialogue.org/documentupload/48345560.pdf

International Institute for Strategic Studies, *The Military Balance 2013*, Vol. 2013, March 2013.

Jason, Michael D., "Integrating the Advisory Effort in the Army: A Full-Spectrum Solution," *Military Review*, September–October 2008, pp. 27–32.

Jourde, Cédric, "Constructing Representations of the 'Global War on Terror' in the Islamic Republic of Mauritania," *Journal of Contemporary African Studies*, Vol. 25, No. 1, 2007, pp. 77–100.

———, "The International Relations of Small Neoauthoritarian States: Islamism, Warlordism, and the Framing of Stability," *International Studies Quarterly*, Vol. 51, No. 2, 2007, pp. 481–503.

———, "Sifting Through the Layers of Insecurity in the Sahel: The Case of Mauritania," Africa Security Brief No. 15, Washington, D.C.: Africa Center for Strategic Studies, National Defense University Press, September 2011.

Khilji, Nasir M., and Ernest M. Zampelli, "The Fungibility of U.S. Military and Non-Military Assistance and the Impacts on Expenditures of Major Aid Recipients," *Journal of Development Economics,* Vol. 43, No. 2, April 1994, pp. 345–362.

Le Sage, Andre, "Africa's Irregular Security Threats: Challenges for U.S. Engagement," Institute for National Strategic Studies, Strategic Forum No. 255, May 2010.

Lugar, Richard G., "Embassies Grapple to Guide Foreign Aid: A Report to Members of the Committee on Foreign Relations," U.S. Senate Foreign Relations Committee, November 2007.

Lyman, Princeton N., "The War on Terrorism in Africa," *Africa in World Politics,* John W. Harbeson and Donald Rothchild, eds., Boulder, Colo.: Westview Press, 2013.

Mackay, Andrew, Mark Sedra, and Geoff Burt, "Security Sector Reform (SSR) in Insecure Environments: Learning from Afghanistan," *Journal of Security Sector Management,* Vol. 8, No. 3, September 2011, pp. 1–20.

Maniruzzaman, Talukder, "Arms Transfers, Military Coups, and Military Rule in Developing States," *Journal of Conflict Resolution,* Vol. 36, No. 4, December 1992, pp. 733–755.

Marshall, Monty G., and Benjamin R. Cole, *Global Report 2011: Conflict, Governance, and State Fragility,* Vienna, Va.: Center for Systemic Peace, 2011.

McCoy, Katherine E., "Trained to Torture? The Human Rights Effects of Military Training at the School of the Americas," *Latin American Perspectives,* Vol. 32, No. 6, November 2005, pp. 47–64.

McNerney, Michael J., Angela O'Mahony, Thomas S. Szayna, Derek Eaton, Caroline Baxter, Colin P. Clarke, Emma Cutrufello, Michael McGee, Heather Peterson, Leslie A. Payne, and Calin Trenkov-Wermuth, *Assessing Security Cooperation as a Preventive Tool,* Santa Monica, Calif.: RAND Corporation, RR-350-A, 2014. As of November 17, 2014:
http://www.rand.org/pubs/research_reports/RR350.html

Mills, Greg "Africa's New Strategic Significance," *Washington Quarterly,* Vol. 27, No. 4, 2004, pp. 157–169.

Moroney, Jennifer D. P., Beth Grill, Joe L. Hogler, Lianne Kennedy-Boudali, and Christopher Paul, *How Successful Are U.S. Efforts to Build Capacity in Developing Countries?: A Framework to Assess the Global Train and Equip "1206" Program*, Santa Monica, Calif.: RAND Corporation, TR-1121-OSD, 2011. As of October 23, 2014:
http://www.rand.org/pubs/technical_reports/TR1121.html

Moroney, Jennifer D. P., David E. Thaler, and Joe Hogler, *Review of Security Cooperation Mechanisms Combatant Commands Utilize to Build Partner Capacity*, Santa Monica, Calif.: RAND Corporation, RR-413-OSD, 2013. As of October 23, 2014:
http://www.rand.org/pubs/research_reports/RR413.html

Nagl, John A., "Institutionalizing Adaptation: It's Time for an Army Advisor Command," *Military Review*, Vol. 88, No. 5, September–October 2008, pp. 21–26.

Nossiter, Adam, Eric Schmitt, and Mark Mazzetti, "French Strikes in Mali Supplant Caution of U.S.," *New York Times*, January 13, 2013. As of October 3, 2014:
http://www.nytimes.com/2013/01/14/world/africa/french-jets-strike-deep-inside-islamist-held-mali.html?pagewanted=1&_r=1&hp&

Oakley, Robert B., and Michael Casey, *The Country Team: Restructuring America's First Line of Engagement*, Strategic Forum No. 227, National Defense University Institute for National Strategic Studies, September 2007.

Office of the Deputy Assistant Secretary of Defense for Plans, *Theater Campaign Planning Planner's Handbook*, version 1.0, February 2012.

Ollivant, Douglas A., "The New U.S. Army/Marine Corps Counterinsurgency Field Manual as Political Science and Political Praxis," *Perspectives on Politics*, Vol. 6, No. 2, June 2008, pp. 357–360.

Organisation for Economic Co-operation and Development, *The Paris Declaration on Aid Effectiveness,* 2005. As of October 3, 2014:
http://www.oecd.org/dac/effectiveness/34428351.pdf

———, *Preventing Violence, War and State Collapse: The Future of Conflict Early Warning and Response*, Paris: OECD Publishing, 2009.

Organisation for Economic Co-operation and Development Development Assistance Committee, *Handbook on Security System Reform: Supporting Security and Justice,* Paris, 2007, pp. 94–96.

———, *Supporting Statebuilding in Situations of Conflict and Fragility*, DAC Guidelines and Reference Series, Paris, 2011.

———, *Accountability and Democratic Governance: Orientations and Principles for Development*, Paris, 2013.

————, "Building Blocks to Prosperity: The Peacebuilding and Statebuilding Goals (PSGs)," Paris, 2012. As of October 2, 2014: http://www.oecd.org/dac/HLM%20one%20pager%20PSGs.pdf

Patrick, Stewart, James Schear, and Mark Wong, *Integrating 21st Century Development and Security Assistance*, Final Report of the Task Force on Nontraditional Security Assistance, Washington, D.C.: Center for Strategic and International Studies, 2008.

Peceny, Mark, "Two Paths to the Promotion of Democracy During U.S. Military Interventions," *International Studies Quarterly*, Vol. 39, No. 3, September 1995, pp. 371–401.

Presidential Policy Directive 23, "Security Sector Assistance." Although the text of the PPD is not publicly available, the document is summarized in White House, Office of the Press Secretary, "Fact Sheet: U.S. Security Sector Assistance Policy," April 5, 2013. As of October 9, 2014: http://www.fas.org/irp/offdocs/ppd/ssa.pdf

Prunier, Gerard, *The Rwanda Crisis*, New York: Columbia University Press, 1996.

Quaranto, Peter J., *Building States While Fighting Terror: Contradictions in United States Strategy in Somalia from 2001 to 2007*, ISS Monograph Series No. 143, Institute for Security Studies, May 2008, p. 55.

Ratner, Ely, "Reaping What You Sow: Democratic Transitions and Foreign Policy Realignment," *Journal of Conflict Resolution*, Vol. 53, No. 3, June 2009, pp. 390–418.

Renou, Xavier, "A New French Policy for Africa?" *Journal of Contemporary African Studies*, Vol. 20, No. 1, 2002, pp. 5–27.

Ruby, Tomislav Z., and Douglas Gibler, "U.S. Professional Military Education and Democratization Abroad," *European Journal of International Relations*, Vol. 16, No. 3, 2010, pp. 339–364.

Saunders, Ken, Bruce Estok, Hayward Hutson, and Tim Watson, "Trainers, Guns and Money: Evolution or Revolution of Global Train and Equip," BiblioScholar, 2012.

Sayigh, Yezid, *Policing the People, Building the State: Authoritarian Transformation in the West Bank and Gaza*, Washington, D.C.: Carnegie Endowment for International Peace, February 2011.

Schmitt, Eric, "Drones in Niger Reflect New U.S. Tack on Terrorism," *New York Times*, July 10, 2013. As of October 2, 2014: http://www.nytimes.com/2013/07/11/world/africa/ drones-in-niger-reflect-new-us-approach-in-terror-fight.html?_r=0

Schnabel, Albrecht, "Ideal Requirements Versus Real Environments in Security Sector Reform," *Security Sector Reform in Challenging Environments*, Geneva: Geneva Centre for the Democratic Control of Armed Forces, 2009.

Sedra, Mark, "Security Sector Reform in Afghanistan and Iraq: Exposing a Concept in Crisis," *Journal of Peacebuilding and Development*, Vol. 3, No. 2, 2007, pp. 7–23.

Serafino, Nina M., *Security Assistance Reform: "Section 1206" Background and Issues for Congress*, Washington, D.C., Congressional Research Service, April 4, 2014.

Serafino, Nina M., Catherine Dale, and Pat Towell, *Building Civilian Interagency Capacity for Missions Abroad: Key Proposals and Issues for Congress*, Washington, D.C., Congressional Research Service, February 9, 2012.

Shinn, David H., "Walking the Line: U.S. Security Policy in East Africa and the Horn," *World Politics Review*, February 20, 2013.

Tarp, Kristoffer N., and Frederik F. Rosén, "Building Civil Servant Capacity in South Sudan," Policy Brief, Danish Institute for International Studies, October 2011.

———, "Coaching and Mentoring for Capacity Development: The Case of South Sudan," *African Security Review*, Vol. 21, No. 1, March 2012, pp. 15–30.

Thompson, Sir Robert, *Defeating Communist Insurgency: The Lessons of Malaya and Vietnam*, St. Petersburg, Fla.: Hailer Publishing, 2005 [1966].

Tisdall, Simon, "Mali: Fragile Democracy and Clumsy U.S. Policy," *The Guardian*, January 18, 2013. As of October 2, 2014:
http://www.theguardian.com/commentisfree/2013/jan/18/
mali-fragile-democracy-clumsy-us-policy

Toft, Monica Duffy, *Securing the Peace: The Durable Settlement of Civil Wars*, Princeton, N.J.: Princeton University Press, 2010.

Tull, Denis M., and Pierre Englebert, "Postconflict Reconstruction in Africa: Flawed Ideas About Failed States," *International Security*, Vol. 32, No. 4, Spring 2008, pp. 106–139.

UK Department for International Development, "Drivers of Change," November 2003. As of October 3, 2014:
http://www.gsdrc.org/docs/open/DOC59.pdf

———, "Political Economy Analysis How To Note," London, July 2009.

United Nations, *Civilian Capacity in the Aftermath of Conflict: Independent Report of the Senior Advisory Group*, 2011.

United Nations Development Programme, *Security Sector Reform and Transitional Justice: A Crisis Post-Conflict Programmatic Approach*, Geneva, March 2003.

———, Bureau for Crisis Prevention and Recovery, *Conflict-Related Development Analysis (CDA)*, Geneva, October 2003.

———, "Institutional and Context Analysis Guidance Note," Geneva, September 2012.

U.S. Agency for International Development, U.S. Department of Defense, and U.S. Department of State, *Security Sector Reform*, February, 2009. As of October 2, 2014:
http://www.state.gov/documents/organization/115810.pdf

————, *Conflict Assessment Framework*, version 2.0, June 2012.

————, Office of Military Affairs, "District Stability Framework," presented at the Military Operations Research Society Mini-Symposium on Social Science Underpinnings of Complex Operations, October 2010.

U.S. Army Training and Doctrine Command, *The U.S. Army Concept for Building Partner Capacity*, Pamphlet 525-8-4, November 22, 2011.

U.S. Department of Defense, *Sustaining U.S. Global Leadership: Priorities for 21st Century Defense*, January 2012.

U.S. Department of Defense and U.S. Department of State Inspectors General, *Interagency Evaluation of the Section 1206 Global Train and Equip Program*, Report No. IE-2009-007/Report No. ISP-I-09-69, August 31, 2009.

U.S. Department of State, Bureau of Arms Control, Verification, and Compliance, International Security Advisory Board, *Report on Security Capacity Building*, January 2013.

U.S. Government Accountability Office, *DoD and State Need to Improve Sustainment Planning and Monitoring and Evaluation for Section 1206 and 1207 Assistance Programs*, Washington, D.C., GAO-10-431, April 15, 2010.

U.S. Joint Chiefs of Staff, Joint Publication 5-0, *Joint Operation Planning*, August 11, 2011.

————, Joint Publication 2-0, *Joint Intelligence*, October 22, 2013.

U.S. Marine Corps, *Implementation of the Regional, Culture, and Language Familiarization Program*, Marine Administrative Message 619/12, October 24, 2012. As of October 7, 2014:
http://www.marines.mil/News/Messages/MessagesDisplay/tabid/13286/Article/129296/implementation-of-the-regional-culture-and-language-familiarization-program.aspx

Van de Walle, Nicolas, *African Economies and the Politics of Permanent Crisis, 1979–1999*, New York: Cambridge University Press, 2001.

————, *Overcoming Stagnation in Aid-Dependent Countries*, Center for Global Development, 2005.

Vogel, Isabel, *Review of the Use of "Theory of Change" in International Development*, UK Department of International Development, April 2012.

Wang, T. Y., "Arms Transfers and Coups d'Etat: A Study on Sub-Saharan Africa," *Journal of Peace Research*, Vol. 35, No. 6, November 1998, pp. 659–675.

Watts, Clint, Jacob Shapiro, and Vahid Brown, *Al-Qa'ida's (Mis)Adventures in the Horn of Africa*, West Point, N.Y.: Combating Terrorism Center, 2007.

Watts, Stephen, Jason H. Campbell, Patrick B. Johnston, Sameer Lalwani, and Sarah H. Bana, *Countering Others' Insurgencies: Understanding U.S. Small-Footprint Interventions in Local Context*, Santa Monica, Calif.: RAND Corporation, RR-513-SRF, 2014. As of November 17, 2014: http://www.rand.org/pubs/research_reports/RR513.html

Whitaker, Beth Elise, "Reluctant Partners: Fighting Terrorism and Promoting Democracy in Kenya," *International Studies Perspectives*, Vol. 9, 2008, pp. 254–271.

White House, *National Security Strategy*, 2010. As of October 2, 2014: http://www.whitehouse.gov/sites/default/files/rss_viewer/national_security_strategy.pdf

———, *National Strategy for Counterterrorism*, 2011. As of October 2, 2014: http://www.whitehouse.gov/sites/default/files/counterterrorism_strategy.pdf

———, *U.S. Strategy Toward Sub-Saharan Africa*, June, 2012. As of October 2, 2014: http://www.state.gov/documents/organization/209377.pdf

White House, Office of the Press Secretary, "Fact Sheet: U.S. Security Sector Assistance Policy," press release, April 5, 2013. As of October 2, 2014: http://www.fas.org/irp/offdocs/ppd/ssa.pdf

Whitlock, Craig, "U.S.-Trained Congolese Troops Committed Rapes and Other Atrocities, U.N. Says," *Washington Post*, May 13, 2013. As of October 3, 2014: http://www.washingtonpost.com/world/national-security/us-trained-congolese-troops-committed-rapes-and-other-atrocities-un-says/2013/05/13/9781dd88-bbfe-11e2-a31d-a41b2414d001_story.html

Wilkason, Colby, and Mikhaila Fogel, "Cartel Weapons and Their Provenance," *The War on Mexican Cartels: Options for U.S. and Mexican Policy-Makers*, Cambridge, Mass.: Harvard University Institute of Politics, September 2012.

Williams, Cindy, and Gordon Adams, *Strengthening Statecraft and Security: Reforming U.S. Planning and Resource Allocation*, Cambridge, Mass.: MIT Security Studies Program, 2008.

World Bank, *Assessing Aid: What Works, What Doesn't, and Why*, Washington, D.C., 1998.

World Bank Public Sector and Governance Group, "Guidance for Supporting State-Building in Fragile and Conflict-Affected States: A Tool-Kit," Washington, D.C., July 12, 2012.

Wuestner, Scott G., *Building Partner Capacity/Security Force Assistance: A New Structural Paradigm*, Carlisle Barracks, Pa.: Strategic Studies Institute, U.S. Army War College, 2009.